Seasonal Kindergarten Units

Mary Phyllis Baumer
Kindergarten Teacher
Fremont Older School
Cupertino Union School District
California

Fearon Publishers, Inc.
Belmont, California

ISBN-0-8224-6330-X

Printed in the United States of America.

Contents

INTRODUCTION 1

UNIT I **FALL** 3
Booklet text 13
Booklet illustrations 17

UNIT II **WINTER** 31
Booklet text 39
Booklet illustrations 43

UNIT III **SPRING** 53
Booklet text 63
Booklet illustrations 67

UNIT IV **SUMMER VACATION** 83
Booklet text 89
Booklet illustrations 93

BIBLIOGRAPHY 103

Introduction

Seasonal Kindergarten Units contains four units, one each for fall, winter, spring, and summer. These units are designed to provide supplementary material to support your art, science, and social studies lessons. The first three units—Fall, Winter, Spring—contain lessons on the weather, animals, birds, plants, trees, and flowers. Unit IV stresses activities for summer vacation and things to look for at the park, the beach, or in the mountains.

Each unit is complete within itself and contains general suggestions for a bulletin board and a display table, plus information and discussion questions for ten lessons, directions for assembling a twenty-page seasonal booklet, and text and illustration patterns for each booklet. Some of the units also contain art projects and songs to teach the class. A bibliography lists suggested books, stories, songs, and films to use for supplementary material and background for each unit.

In addition to the logical, factual information gained from the units, the child also learns about the sequencing of a book through the assembly of the seasonal booklet. He gains knowledge about how to use a book and learns that books contain consecutive information. Through the construction of his booklet, the child discovers that every book has a title that tells what kind of "story" is inside. He also learns that a book is opened from the cover with the title on it and is read page by page, from the front to the back.

The text material and the illustrations for the children's booklets are located at the end of each unit. The teacher should make duplicator masters using these patterns, duplicate the text and art, and pass out the appropriate material daily. If an art page contains objects that are to appear on several different booklet pages, she should cut apart the pieces so that the child gets only the object needed for that day's lesson. For example, the brown page may have art for booklet pages 6, 8, and 10. In this case, the teacher should cut the page apart and hand out the art for page 6. The child is to do the cutting around the outline of the art. The color to be used for the illustrations is specified on each page. If colored paper is in short supply, duplicate the art on manilla or white paper and let the children color the illustrations. The children are to cut apart the text and paste it on the left-hand page and cut out the accompanying illustration and paste it on the right-hand page. These cutting and pasting experiences help develop the ability to follow directions and further the development of eye-hand coordination.

As the child assembles his booklet, stress the use of the *next* page so that he does not skip around and spoil the sequence. By pasting the text on the left and the picture on the right, the child should learn that there is a relationship between pictures and the printed word.

UNIT I

Fall

The purpose of this unit is to make children aware of the effect of fall seasonal changes on plants, trees, animals, and the weather. This will be accomplished through the use of a bulletin board, science table, discussion questions, and the compilation of a fall booklet.

Set the atmosphere for your fall unit by creating an appropriate bulletin board using typical fall colors and pictures. Have a variety of pictures representative of fall—migrating birds, a school and school bus, fruits and vegetables, a Halloween jack-o'-lantern, and a Thanksgiving turkey, for example. For added interest, mount these pictures on large leaf shapes cut from red, green, yellow, orange, and brown construction paper.

In addition to the bulletin board, set up an attractive science table display of objects the children can handle. Leaves, seeds, nuts, fruits, vegetables, and stuffed toy animals such as squirrels and bears might make an interesting display. The class can take a "fall walk" together to find suitable objects for the science table, or the children can bring objects from home and share them with their classmates.

Before starting class discussion, assemble these materials for making the fall booklets:

1. Scissors.
2. Paste.
3. For each child, enough 9″ x 12″ construction paper to make a twenty-page booklet plus front and back cover.

4. A supply of different colored construction paper for making the duplicates of the illustrations. If colored paper is not available, run the dittos on white or manilla construction paper and have the children color them.
5. Duplicate copies of the text and the illustrations that accompany it for each child (*see* pages 13-30).

LESSON ONE

Begin your first lesson with some general discussion about the seasons. Have the children name the four seasons.

1. Discuss the meaning of the word *season*.
2. Ask what season has just passed.
3. What season is beginning now?
4. How do we know that fall is beginning? (School has begun. Leaves are turning colors. We see pumpkins, apples, and squash in the store or garden. It is getting dark earlier. The air is getting colder. We need to wear sweaters and heavier clothing.)
5. Discuss how the children get to school.
6. How should children act on a school bus?
7. If most of the children walk to school, discuss being careful on the way to and from school.

After some introductory discussion about the season, hold up a blank booklet. It should have **Fall** written on the front of it and your name in one corner. Point to the word *Fall* and explain that it is the title of the book. Discuss the meaning of *title* and point out that the title of a book is always on the front cover of the book. Lead into a discussion of how a book is opened and read—starting from the front. Explain to the children that the pages go in order.

Demonstrate this by cutting out the text for page 1 and pasting it onto the left-hand page. Then cut out the school bus and paste it on the right-hand page. Show your booklet to the children and then pass out duplicated copies of the text and illustration. Direct the children to cut out the school bus and to cut apart the text for the first day. When everyone has finished cutting, collect the remaining text on the page. Pass out a booklet to each child and have him print the title and his name on the cover. Discuss which is the left-hand page, which is the right-hand page, and the top and bottom of each page. Have the children paste down the text and the illustration, checking to be sure that each child pastes on the correct pages. Read the text to the children as they follow along in their booklets.

If most of the children walk to school, devote an extra page to a hand-drawn picture of a child walking.

LESSON TWO

Review the previous day's information and ask for any science table additions. Ask if anyone would like to "read" yesterday's story from his booklet. Then begin today's discussion about the weather.

1. Discuss the kinds of weather—cloudy, rainy, sunny, windy, cold, warm, etc.
2. With a flashlight and a globe, show how the sun warms the earth in varying degrees according to the tilt of the earth toward and away from the sun. In fall, temperatures begin to cool as our part of the earth tilts away from the sun.
3. Point out that it is colder in the early morning and late afternoon.
4. Discuss fall in your state or area and compare it with other parts of the country. This is a good time to display a United States map.
5. What kind of clothing do we need now?
6. Do boys and girls in all parts of the country need warmer clothing in the fall?
7. Since the days are getting shorter, children cannot play outside as long.

Have the children cut apart the text and paste it on page 3 of their booklets. Next, they should cut out the paper doll and paste it on page 4. Then, they should cut out the clothes and paste them on the doll. Each child can create a face for the doll and add ears and some hair. As the children paste, check to see that they are using consecutive pages of their booklets. Read the text to the children when every child has finished pasting.

LESSON THREE

Review the previous day's lesson. Ask for someone to "read" the first two lessons. Then begin the day's lesson on plants. Discuss the fact that some plants "sleep" in the fall and bloom in the spring. Read the book *Tulips* by John Peterson, from the Little Owl collection of books (Holt, Rinehart & Winston, Inc.). Have a bulb to show to the children.

1. Hold up the bulb and ask if anyone knows what it is.
2. Ask what it is for.
3. After establishing that it is a bulb, ask if all bulbs grow into the same kind of flowers.
4. What kinds of flowers grow from bulbs? (Tulip, daffodil, crocus, for example.) Differentiate between flowers that sprout from seeds (daisy, zinnia, bachelor button, pansy, for example) and ones that grow from bulbs.
5. When must a bulb be planted? (In the fall for spring bloom and in early spring for summer or fall bloom.)

For the lesson, the children will be cutting out a brown bulb, one green flower stem with leaves, and their choice of a red tulip or a yellow daffodil. Since all of these objects appear on pages with other shapes, the teacher should cut the sheets apart and pass out the objects to the children. The children can then cut around the outline of the appropriate shapes. In this way, the girls and boys won't accidentally spoil one of the dittoed sheets.

Plant some bulbs and place the container on the science table. Have the children take turns watering the bulbs. Keep track of the time the bulbs "sleep" by marking the days on a calendar.

LESSON FOUR

Review the information learned in the first three days. Ask for a volunteer to "read" the previous day's story. Talk about leaves today. Introduce the discussion with the questions that follow.

1. Who has noticed what is happening to the leaves?
2. When do the leaves start to fall off the trees?
3. What colors do the leaves turn before they fall?
4. Why do they turn different colors? (Explain that a leaf is made up of veins and cells. The veins give moisture to the leaf and the cells produce food. As the leaf gets older and as fall approaches, the veins fill up near the stem of the leaf. It loses its green color and turns red, yellow, and orange. Finally, it dries up completely and falls off the tree.)
5. Explain that a new leaf bud will replace the old leaf, but that the tree "sleeps" until spring when the new leaves grow.

Have the children cut out the text for page 7 and paste it down. Then direct them to cut out the brown tree trunk and the red, yellow, brown, green, and orange leaves and paste them on page 8. Again, the teacher should first cut the shapes apart and pass out only those to be used for this lesson. The children can then cut out the outline of the leaves, etc. Read the text to them.

Art Projects _____

Make some **sponge-painted leaves** using manilla or white drawing paper, thick red, yellow, orange, and brown poster paint, leaf patterns made of cardboard, and small pieces of sponge. Using a different sponge for each color, sponge all colors of the paint over the paper. When dry, turn the paper over and draw around the leaf patterns. Cut out the leaves and use them on a bulletin board. They could be pinned at random over the board or placed at the top of a large cutout tree trunk mounted on the board. As winter approaches, the leaves could fall from the tree.

Make a **leaf puppet** using the pattern at the end of this unit. Each child should have a pattern on green construction paper and another pattern on his choice of any fall color. The children should cut out and assemble the puppets as shown here. Let the children dance the puppets up and down as they sing the leaf song, using first the green one and then the colored one.

Little Green Leaf

I am a lit- tle green leaf you see. I

grow all spring and sum- mer on a tree. But

in the fall I go down down down in my

love- ly dress, red, yel- low, and brown.

LESSON FIVE

Go over what was discussed previously. Have someone "read" the story about the leaves. Then use the following questions to introduce today's lesson about fruits that grow and ripen in the fall.

1. Ask if anyone knows what *ripe* means. Explain and demonstrate by holding up a ripe fruit and an unripe one.

2. Ask who likes apples.
3. What colors do apples turn in the fall? (Yellow or red.)
4. Talk about how apples are good to eat.
5. Explain what the core is and how new trees grow from apple seeds.
6. How were apples first grown? Talk about Johnny Appleseed. Show the film *Johnny Appleseed,* available from Denoyer-Geppert, 5235 Ravenswood Ave., Chicago, Ill. 60640.
7. What does mother or grandmother make with apples?
8. Do pears get ripe in the fall? (Yes. Winter Nelis, Anjou, for example.)

If possible, show the children different kinds of apples and pears and let them taste each kind. Then, let the children cut out the text and the green, red, and yellow apples and paste them on pages 9 and 10. The teacher should cut apart the green, yellow, and red sheets and hand out only the apples for the children to cut out.

LESSON SIX

Follow the usual procedure for review and then begin the day's discussion of vegetables using the questions that follow.

1. What kinds of vegetables get ripe in the fall? (Squash, pumpkins, radishes, spinach, Chinese cabbage, rutabagas.)
2. Jack-o'-lanterns are made from pumpkins. What else is made from pumpkins?
3. What can you do with the seeds?
4. How many of you like squash? It is a fall vegetable.

It would be helpful if you show the children a pumpkin and a squash as you talk about them. When you feel the children are ready, have them cut out the text, the yellow and green squash, and the pumpkin. The text should be pasted on page 11 and the illustrations on page 12.

LESSON SEVEN

Review the previous day's lessons. After a volunteer has "read" the text, talk about how fall is Halloween time. Introduce the day's lesson with these questions and discussion topics.

1. What do we make out of pumpkins for Halloween?
2. When are pumpkin seeds planted? (April or May in the southern U.S. and May or June in the northern U.S.)
3. Discuss saftey with matches when lighting a jack-o'-lantern.
4. Talk about Halloween costumes. Ask each child about his costume.

With the children's help, make a jack-o'-lantern for your room. Then have the children cut out the text for page 13 of their booklets and the picture of the jack-o'-lantern for page 14. You may want the children to draw their own jack-o'-lanterns rather than using the pattern. When the children have completed pasting, read the text to them.

Art Projects

Make a **paper-bag pumpkin** using a small paper bag, orange, green, and black poster paint, and newspapers. Stuff the paper bag with crumpled newspaper. Twist the top of the bag so that it stays closed, or fasten it with a piece of string or a rubber band. Paint all of the bag except the twisted top with thick orange paint. Paint the top green. After the orange paint has dried, use the black paint to add a face.

Create a **pumpkin man** from orange and black construction paper. Fold one sheet of 9″ x 12″ orange construction paper in half. Draw a pumpkin shape on one side and then cut out the shape. Unfold the paper and paste on a face made from scraps of black paper. Make strips of orange paper into springs for the arms and legs by folding them back and forth. Cut hands and feet from scraps and paste them to the ends of the springs. Paste the arms and legs to the pumpkin face as shown in the illustration.

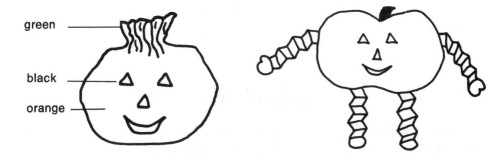

LESSON EIGHT

After reviewing previous lessons and having a child tell the story, discuss where birds go in the fall. Use a map to show migration routes. Discuss north, south, east, and west, and the variation in climates. Ask the children to point out where they live on the map and then ask these questions.

1. Why do birds go away in the fall? (The weather is getting too cool for them. Food is harder to find.)
2. Where do they go? (South—some go to Mexico and South America.)
3. Why do birds fly south? (Because they are looking for a warmer climate.)
4. Do all birds go away? Which ones do; which ones don't? (No. Chickadees, jays, orioles, house sparrows, downy woodpeckers, and cardinals

don't migrate; robins, blackbirds, **hummingbirds**, house wrens, and geese do, for example.)

5. When do birds come back? Why? (In the spring. Because it is getting warmer, more food is available, and they know it is time to build a nest and raise young.)

Show the children pictures of various birds, including ducks, that fly south. Take a bird walk now and later in the fall and have the children keep a class record of birds seen.

Supervise the children as they cut out the text and the picture of the bluebird and paste them onto pages 15 and 16.

Art Project _____

Make large **geese patterns** two feet long. Have the children trace around the patterns on heavy gray paper and cut out the shapes. Hang these paper geese by threads from the ceiling, arranging them in a V formation.

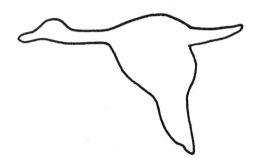

LESSON NINE

After reviewing the previous lessons, talk about squirrels and how they get ready for winter. Use these discussion questions.

1. How many of you have seen a squirrel?
2. Where did you see a squirrel?
3. Do we see many in the city?
4. Where do squirrels live? (In holes under the ground or in hollows of trees.)
5. What do they eat? (Nuts, grain, bird eggs, insects, fruit.)
6. What do they collect and store for the winter? (Nuts, especially pine nuts and acorns.)
7. What does a squirrel do in the winter? (Squirrels wrap their tails around themselves for a blanket and sleep most of the winter.)
8. Do you think squirrels ever forget where they hide their nuts? Discuss how squirrels help with reforestation by forgetting where nuts are buried.

Read this poem, which comes from Volume 1 of *Childcraft* (Field Educational Enterprises, Inc., 1949, anonymous).

Whisky, Frisky

Whisky, frisky,
Hippity hop,
Up he goes
To the tree top!

Whirly, twirly,
Round and round.
Down he scampers
To the ground.

Furly, curly,
What a tail!
Tall as a feather,
Broad as a sail!

Where's his supper?
In the shell.
Snappity, crackity,
Out it fell!

Read *Perri,* by Felix Salten (Golden Press—Western Publishing Company, Inc.).

Have the children cut out the text and the picture of the squirrel and paste them on pages 17 and 18 of their booklets. Read the text to the children and discuss it, if necessary.

LESSON TEN

Review the previous lesson. Tell the children that today they are going to learn about animals that hibernate. Explain the word to the children.

1. Why do you think animals hibernate? (They can't find enough food. They can't stand the cold.)
2. Can you think of a big, furry animal that hibernates? (Bear.)
3. How do bears keep warm when they hibernate? (They have put on an extra layer of fat and they find a hole or cave to sleep in.)
4. How do they stay alive without food? (Bears have a layer of fat under their skins. As hibernation time approaches, bears eat more to build up the fat layer. The fat layer keeps them alive while they hibernate.)

5. Who or what tells bears when it is time to hibernate? (They always go to hibernate on about the same day every fall unless the weather is unseasonably warm. Nobody is sure how a bear knows it is time to hibernate or how birds can tell when to migrate. Perhaps weather changes trigger their instincts.)

Have the children cut out the picture of the bear and the accompanying text and paste them on pages 19 and 20 of their booklets. The back cover should be blank. Read the text to the children and discuss it if they wish.

The season called **summer** has just ended.

The season called **fall**, or **autumn**, has begun.

It is time for school again.

Our big brothers and sisters go to school on the big yellow bus.

This year, we are going to school on the big yellow bus, too.

------------------------------ cut here—page 1 ------------------------------

In the fall, days get colder.

We must wear sweaters and jackets.

Boys wear long pants.

It is cold early in the morning.

It is cold in the late afternoon.

It gets dark early. So, we cannot play outdoors as long.

------------------------------ cut here—page 3 ------------------------------

We plant bulbs in the fall.

Bulbs are usually rounded and brownish in color.

When it is spring, they will grow into flowers.

Tulips of many different colors grow from bulbs.

Daffodils and other kinds of flowers grow from bulbs, too.

------------------------------ cut here—page 5 ------------------------------

In October, the weather gets colder.

Tree leaves are beginning to turn **red, orange, yellow, and
brown.**

Soon they will fall off the trees.

Down, down to the ground they fall.

Have you noticed how the trees **are changing colors?**

- cut here—page 7 -

Apples get ripe in the fall.

There are red apples called Delicious.

There are yellow apples called Delicious, too.

There are red apples called Jonathans.

There are green apples called Pippins.

Mother sometimes makes pies out **of apples.**

- -cut here—page 9 -

In October, the pumpkins and squash that were planted in
the spring start to get ripe.

Have you ever grown pumpkins **and squash in your garden?**

Mother makes pies out of the **pumpkins.**

She cooks the squash for dinner.

- cut here—page 11 -

Fall is Halloween time, too.

Halloween is on the last day of October, the 31st.

Let's make a jack-o'-lantern out of a big orange pumpkin.

We can put a candle inside our jack-o'-lantern.

The face lights up when the candle is lighted.

------------------------------ cut here—page 13 ------------------------------

In the fall, some birds begin to get cold.

They cannot find enough food to eat.

They fly south where it is warm and there is plenty of food.

They stay there until spring.

Then, they fly north and stay until the weather turns cold
again.

------------------------------ cut here—page 15 ------------------------------

Squirrels are small furry animals.

They like to eat nuts and berries.

Squirrels store food for the winter.

They hide nuts in tree hollows or bury them in the ground.

Sometimes they forget where they put the nuts.

Then, a tree may grow from one of the nuts.

------------------------------ cut here—page 17 ------------------------------

In the fall, bears go to sleep.

This is called hibernating.

They sleep all winter.

Before they go to sleep, they eat a lot of food.

The food makes a layer of fat under their skin.

This fat keeps them alive while they hibernate.

- cut here—page 19 -

yellow

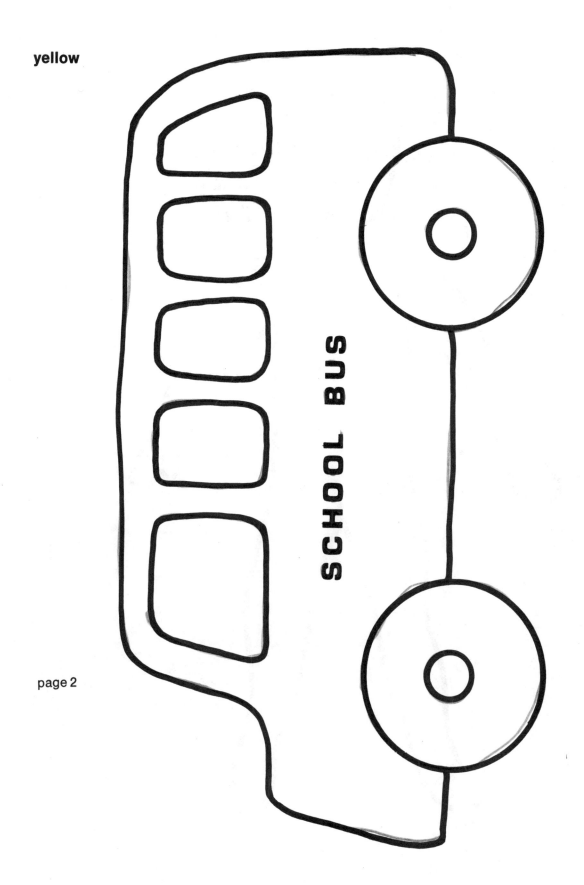

SCHOOL BUS

page 2

17

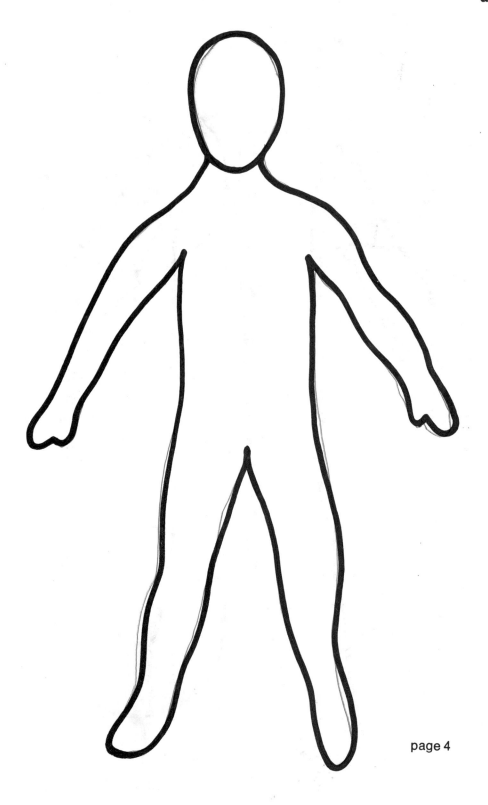

page 4

any color

page 4

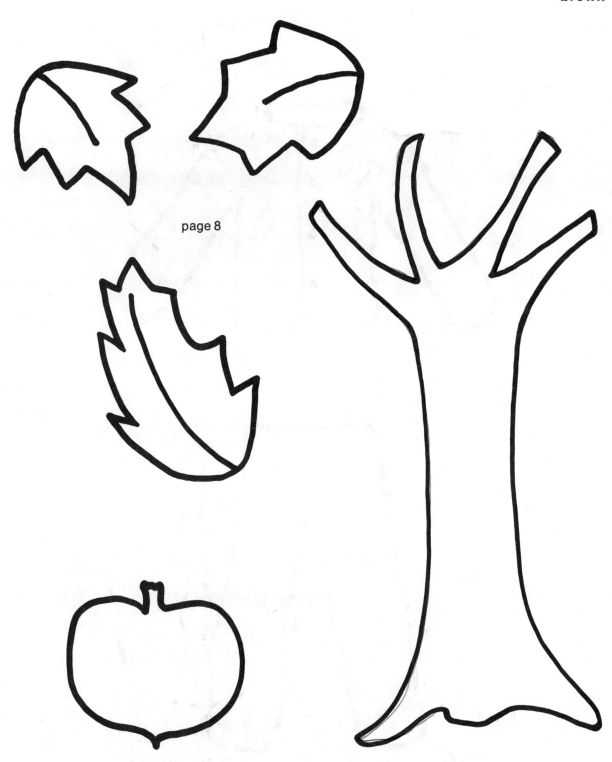

page 8

page 6

page 8

green

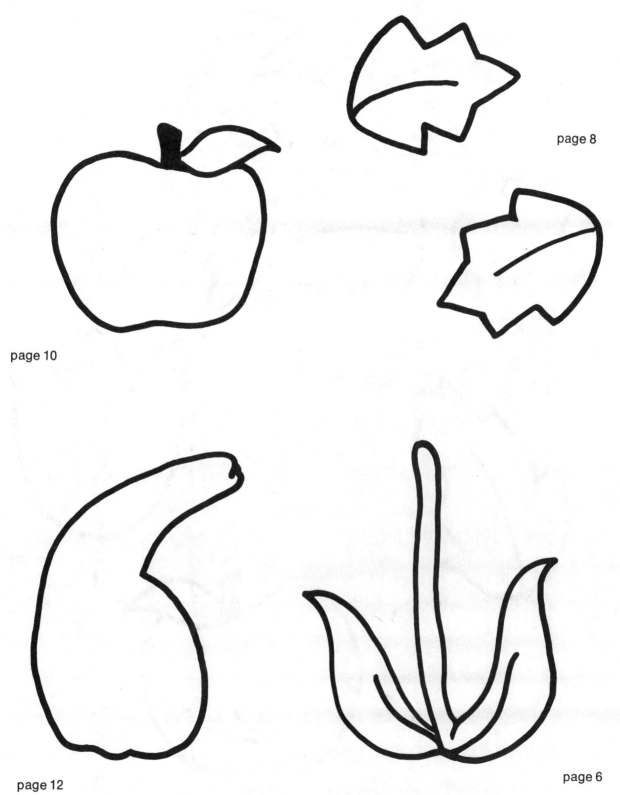

page 8

page 10

page 12

page 6

21

page 8

page 6

page 10

yellow

page 8

page 10

page 12

page 6

23

orange

page 12

page 8

orange

page 14

page 16

brown or gray

page 18

27

page 20

LESSON FOUR

string hole

attach arm

attach **arm**

attach leg

attach leg

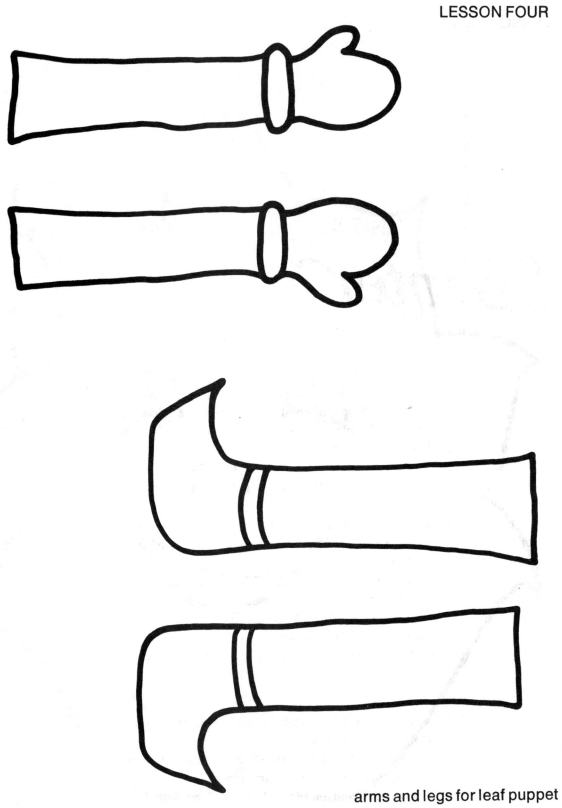

arms and legs for leaf puppet

UNIT II

Winter

The purpose of this unit is to make children aware of the effect of winter seasonal changes on animals, plants, trees, and the weather. It should also help them realize that winter does not have the same conditions in all parts of the United States. The same methods as in Unit I—a bulletin board, display table, discussion, and compilation of a booklet—will be used to accomplish these purposes.

The bulletin board might display winter pictures mounted on colored paper. Try to have a variety of pictures depicting winter conditions in all parts of the United States.

For the science display table, have dried fall leaves that can be crunched in the hand, a bare tree branch, dolls dressed in warm clothes, and an umbrella. Set up a globe and a flashlight so children can use it themselves after Lesson 4 on why it gets dark earlier.

These materials will be needed for making the winter booklet.

1. Scissors.
2. Paste.
3. A blank 9″ x 12″ construction paper booklet containing twenty pages and having front and back covers.
4. A supply of 9″ x 12″ construction paper of appropriate colors to be used for making duplicates of the illustrations.
5. A duplicate of the text and of the pictures that go with it for each child. These will be given out daily.

LESSON ONE

Ask for a volunteer to name the four seasons before starting the first lesson. Review the meaning of the word *season*.

1. Ask what season has just gone by.
2. What season is beginning now?
3. How do we know that winter is beginning? (Trees are bare. It is colder. It may be rainy, snowy, icy, or warm and sunny depending on the location in the U.S. Most birds are gone. We must wear warmer clothes. It gets dark earlier.)
4. How long did fall last? What months are fall months?
5. How long do you think winter will last? Name the winter months.
6. What do we wear on our hands to keep them warm in winter? Children in warmer climates may need a comprehensive explanation of why mittens are necessary. Let them feel ice cubes to get an idea of how cold snow is.

Follow the same procedure for introducing the booklet as in Unit I. Review the meaning of *title, front, back, top, bottom, left-hand page,* and *right-hand page.*

Demonstrate with a blank booklet that has **Winter** written on the front cover and your name in the lower left-hand corner. Cut out the text and paste it on the left-hand page. Then cut out the paper doll and paste it on the right-hand page. Cut out the snowsuit, hat, boots, and mittens and paste them on top of the doll. Add eyes, nose, mouth, ears, and a little hair with crayons. Stress pasting the text and accompanying illustrations in order on consecutive pages. Read the text to the children and then direct them to cut and paste in their own booklets.

LESSON TWO

Review the previous lesson. Ask for someone to "read" the text from his booklet. Then begin today's lesson.

1. Ask if winter is always cold everywhere. Locate on the United States map where it is usually cold and where it is warm.
2. Do all people wear warm clothes in the winter? Have a child point to a state where heavy, warm clothes would be worn.
3. Ask a child to point to a state where a person might wear summer-type clothes in the winter.
4. Can children swim, play baseball, and ride bikes in the winter in some places?
5. Where would you rather live in the winter—where it is cold or where it is hot? Why?

On page 3 of the booklet the children should paste the text. Then they should paste the cutout paper doll on page 4. Direct them to cut out the shorts and T-shirt and paste them on top of the doll. They should be encouraged to add hair, ears, eyes, nose, and mouth to the paper cutout with crayons. Review how to open and use a book, and read the text to them.

LESSON THREE

Discuss the previous lesson and then ask for a volunteer to "read" the text. Today's lesson continues the discussion about weather and focuses on rain as a type of winter weather.

1. Ask what kinds of winter weather there can be in the United States. (Warm, cool, cold, snow, rain.)
2. Discuss rain as a kind of winter weather. Point out on the map where it rains in the winter. (Coastal California, Oregon, and Washington, for example.)
3. What do we wear to keep dry?
4. What might happen if we get wet feet?
5. Ask the children if they would like to keep a record of the weather. Prepare a large piece of paper by ruling it into columns for recording the date, day of the week, whether it was rainy and cool, warm and sunny, cold and snowy, etc. Explain to the children that this is called a *weather chart*.

Have the group cut out and paste the paper doll on page 6 and the text on page 5. They should cut out the raincoat, hat, and boots and paste them on the paper doll. If they wish, they may draw an umbrella.

LESSON FOUR

Follow the established procedure for review and then begin the day's lesson with these questions.

1. Are days longer or shorter in winter? Why? (The earth slants away from the sun so that the sun appears later in the morning and "sets" sooner in the evening.) Demonstrate this, using a flashlight as the sun and a ball or world globe.
2. Do you know which is the shortest day of the year? (December 22 is generally recognized as the shortest.)
3. Has the weather changed since school began? How?
4. Do you think there might be a place where the sun never shines in winter? Is there a place where the sun shines all night in winter? (Explain about northern Norway, Greenland, and the Antarctic Circle.)

Have the children cut out the two clock faces and the two sun faces. They should paste the 7:00 clock beside the wide-awake sun and the 5:00 clock beside the sleepy sun. The cutout text goes on page 7.

LESSON FIVE

Review Lesson 6 and have someone "read" the text. Today discuss snow, using the map to show where it snows in the winter.

1. Ask if the children have ever been tobogganing.
2. What other things can you do outside after it snows?
3. What do you think snow is?
4. How cold does it have to be before it snows?
5. Why do you think it snows in some parts of the country but not in others?
6. How does snow make it difficult for animals? (They have trouble finding food and keeping warm.)

Direct the children to cut out and paste the text on page 9 and the snowman on page 10. Let them draw a hat, arms, eyes, nose, mouth, and buttons with a black crayon. A scarf may be added if desired.

Art Projects _____

A **snowman** can be made from different-sized bags obtained at a bakery or a grocery store. Each child will need two bags, two sheets of newspaper, a 6" x 6" circle of black paper, one 3" x 4" piece of black paper, scissors, string, paste, and red ribbon or yarn cut into an 8" length.

Crumple two sheets of newspaper separately. Stuff one sheet into each of the white paper bags. Twist the top of one bag to keep it closed, turn it upside down, and insert it into the top of the other bag. Tie a string tightly around the bags.

Crease the 3″ side of the 3″ x 4″ paper about ⅓ of the way up. Paste it in the middle of the circle. Then paste this on the top bag to make the hat. Use scraps of black paper to make eyes, nose, mouth, and buttons. Tie the ribbon or string on for a scarf.

Let each child make a **snow picture.** For this project, you will need one piece of 12″ x 18″ black or blue construction paper for each child, an electric mixer, liquid starch, a large box of Tide detergent, and Ivory or Lux flakes (optional).

In a large mixing bowl, beat together one cup liquid starch and two cups Tide. Add water as you beat until the mixture is the consistency of whipped cream. For 9″ x 12″ paper, give each child one tablespoonful; for 12″ x 18″ paper, dip out two tablespoonsful. Direct them to use their fingers to paint a snow scene. Tell them not to cover all of the paper. They should leave a bare space for the sky. For added sparkle, they can sprinkle soap flakes onto the picture before it has dried.

LESSON SIX

Review Lesson 5 and have a volunteer "read" the text from his booklet. Tell the children that today's lesson is about animals that hibernate. Review the meaning of *hibernate* before going on to the questions.

1. We have learned about one animal that hibernates. Which one?
2. Do your pets have to hibernate? Why not?
3. Can you name other animals that hibernate? (Skunks, woodchucks, and squirrels hibernate, but because of their smaller size, they wake up once in a while to eat. Frogs and toads hibernate in the mud at the bottom of lakes and ponds.)
4. Do zoo animals hibernate? Why? (No. They have enough food to eat.)

Pass out duplicates of the squirrel and frog and the text for page 11. Direct the children to cut out and paste the text on the left-hand page and the squirrel and frog on the right-hand page. Stress the use of the next page. Read the text to the children before going on to the next lesson.

LESSON SEVEN

Follow the usual procedure for review. Then explain that some animals do not have to hibernate during the winter. The children should volunteer the information that their pets don't hibernate.

1. Ask if they can think of any other animals that do not hibernate. (Rabbits, deer, foxes, and weasels, for example.)
2. What do these animals eat during the winter? (Tree bark, grass, berries, other small animals.)
3. Explain that some animals' coats change color during the winter. In this way, they can hide from other animals. (The fur of some rabbits turns white so that they cannot be seen against the snow. The weasel's fur turns white also, and he is then known as an *ermine*. People used to like coats made from ermine fur.)
4. Ask if anyone knows what a weasel looks like. Show pictures of one in its summer and winter coats.

Have the children cut out and paste the rabbit onto the right-hand page and the correct text on the left.

LESSON EIGHT

After reviewing the information from the previous lesson, ask for someone to "read" from his booklet. Explain that today you are going to talk about birds that do not migrate during the winter.

1. Ask if they remember learning about birds that do migrate. It may be necessary to explain the meaning of *migrate* again and to review Lesson 8 of Unit I before proceeding.
2. Talk about winter birds such as woodpeckers and nuthatches. Read "The Chickadee" from *Johnny and the Birds,* by Ian Munn (Rand McNally & Co.) and *Birds in Winter,* by Allen Eitzen from the Little Owl Series (Holt, Rinehart & Winston, Inc.).
3. What do winter birds eat? (Small seeds from various cones, insects, nuts, and berries.)
4. What would you put on a feeding station for birds? (Peanut butter, raisins, breadcrumbs, birdseed, sunflower seeds, and suet are good things to put out in winter.)

Have the children cut out and paste the feeding station onto page 16 of their booklets and paste the correct text on page 15. They can cut out and paste the bird on the feeding station or draw their own birds. If desired, have the children color in typical chickadee markings such as the black cap and the black spot under the head.

Art Project _____

Make a simple **feeding station** from a pinecone. Ask each child to bring in a pinecone, or provide cones for the children. Have a supply of sunflower seeds, birdseed, raisins, suet, peanut butter, and breadcrumbs available. Show the children how to stuff these things into the cracks of their pinecones. Attach a string to the top of each cone and let the children take their feeders home. If possible, put a feeder up outside your classroom window so the children can watch birds.

If pinecones aren't readily available, make a feeder out of two pieces of wood. One piece should be wide enough to form a suitable platform. The seeds, etc., should be placed on this platform. Caution the children to place their feeders out of the reach of cats.

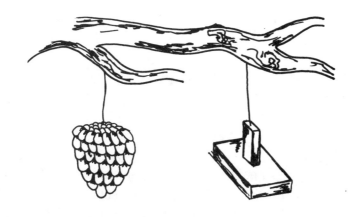

LESSON NINE

Discuss weather in all parts of the United States in winter—warm, cold, rainy, snowy. Then, talk about plants and winter weather.

1. Ask the child what becomes of plants and flowers in the winter. Explain that in cold, rainy, and snowy areas, plants and flowers usually do not bloom or grow in the winter. Some bushes lose their leaves like trees, and most plants "sleep" all winter. Plants must have warm weather in order to have leaves and flowers.

2. Now, think about what you just heard. Can flowers grow and bloom where it is cold and snowy? Why not? Can flowers grow and bloom where it is cold and rainy? Why not?

3. If we planted seeds in the cold winter ground, what do you think would happen? This could be done as a science experiment. Plant some seeds outdoors in the winter and again in the spring. Seeds can also be planted in pots inside to see if they will grow where the climate is correct.

4. What do you think happens to plants in winter in the warmer, southern part of the United States? (They bloom and grow all the year around.)
5. In the winter, plants can be grown in greenhouses. These are usually made of glass or plastic and are kept warm with heaters. Lights are turned on inside so that all the plants will think they are in the sun. Both flowers and vegetables are grown all winter in greenhouses.
6. At Christmastime, we see many poinsettias. These come from Mexico and the southern part of the United States. We think of them as a winter flower and like to use them at Christmas because they have pretty red blossoms. They bloom in winter because they are grown in greenhouses. If they are planted outside, they bloom in early spring.

Cut out the poinsettia blossom and the leaves and paste them on the right-hand page. The text goes on page 17. Lines on the leaves and the blossom should be drawn in later so that children won't become confused and accidentally cut on them.

LESSON TEN

Again, discuss winter weather in our United States. Review what happened to the trees in the fall.

1. What do you think happens to trees in the winter? If trees grew leaves in winter, what might happen to them? (Wind might blow them off. They would freeze and die because of cold.)
2. What is sap? What happens to sap in the winter? (Trees have sap inside that runs all through them like our blood. The sap slows down in the winter. In the northeastern part of the United States, Sugar Maple trees grow. Just as winter is ending and the sap is beginning to move again, people poke a hole in the tree bark. They collect the sap in buckets and make maple syrup and maple sugar from it. This was the only kind of sugar the Pilgrims had.)
3. Some trees do not lose their leaves in the fall. These trees are green all winter. Which trees do not lose their leaves? (Evergreen trees.)
4. What do we use evergreen trees for in the winter? (Christmas trees.) What do we call their leaves? (Needles.)
5. Trees grow new leaves in the spring. They need warmer weather for the leaves to come out. Fruit trees get blossoms first and then fruit and leaves. Why can't fruit grow on fruit trees in the winter? (Too cold.) When do we see fruit on fruit trees? (In the summer and fall.)

Have the children paste the text on the left-hand page. Then they should cut out the evergreen tree and paste it on page 20. Each child can decorate his tree using scraps of different colored paper or crayons. Read the text to the children.

Now it is winter.

This is the time of year when it is cold in some parts of the world.

It snows a lot when it is cold.

Some boys and girls must wear boots and coats or snowsuits.

--------------------------------- cut here—page 1 ------------------------------

In some parts of our country it is warm in the winter.

Florida is one state where it is usually warm in the winter.

It is usually warm in southern California, too.

Boys and girls can often go swimming in the winter in Florida.

They can wear shorts and T-shirts, too.

--------------------------------- cut here—page 3 ------------------------------

In some parts of our country it does not snow in the winter.

It rains instead of snowing.

When it rains, we must wear a raincoat, hat, and boots.

We carry an umbrella, too.

Sometimes, for fun, we call an umbrella a "bumbershoot."

--------------------------------- cut here—page 5 ------------------------------

In the winter, the sun gets up late.

So, it doesn't start to get light until around seven o'clock
  in the morning.

The sun goes to bed early in the winter.

So, it gets dark around five o'clock.

--------------------------------cut here—page 7--------------------------------

We call him a man.

But he is not a real man.

Sometimes he is thin and sometimes he is fat.

He wears a hat on his head.

When the sun comes out, he disappears.

Who is he?

--------------------------------cut here—page 9--------------------------------

When it turns cold, some animals find a cave or hole to
  sleep in.

They go to sleep for the whole winter.

This is called *hibernating*.

They hibernate because they cannot find food.

They hibernate because it is cold outside, too.

Bears, squirrels, skunks, woodchucks, frogs, and toads
  hibernate in the winter.

--------------------------------cut here—page 11--------------------------------

Rabbits do not hibernate in the winter.

They must hunt very hard for food.

Sometimes, when it snows, the only food a rabbit can find is the bark of a tree.

The fur of some rabbits turns white in the winter.

This helps them hide from other animals.

-------------------------------cut here—page 13-------------------------------

Some birds do not fly south when winter comes.

One of these is the chickadee.

Sometimes birds cannot find enough food in the winter.

You can help the birds by putting out food for them.

Make a feeding station of wood or a pinecone.

Then put out raisins, birdseed, breadcrumbs, suet, and sunflower seeds for the birds.

-------------------------------cut here—page 15-------------------------------

Poinsettias are plants that are usually seen at Christmastime.

Their pretty blossoms are red and their leaves are green.

Poinsettias are grown in greenhouses in the winter.

Men use heaters and lights to keep the plants warm.

In winter, the air and the ground are too cold for plants to grow outdoors.

-------------------------------cut here—page 17-------------------------------

Most trees drop their leaves in the fall.
In winter, their branches are bare.
Some trees have needles instead of leaves.
These trees are called evergreen trees.
They do not lose their needles in winter.
We use evergreen trees for Christmas trees.

------------------------------ cut here—page 19 ------------------------------

any color

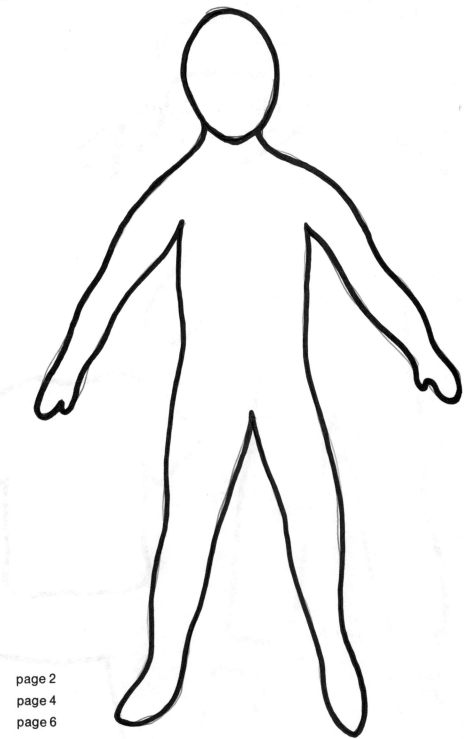

page 2
page 4
page 6

Note: This page should be duplicated *three* times for each child.

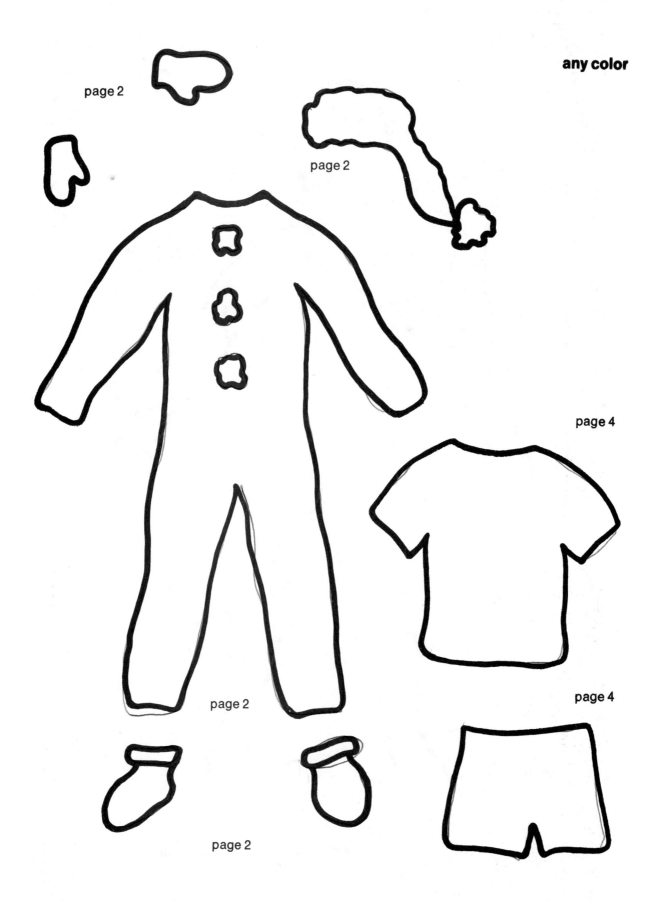

any color

page 2

page 2

page 4

page 2

page 4

page 2

44

red

page 18

page 6

page 6

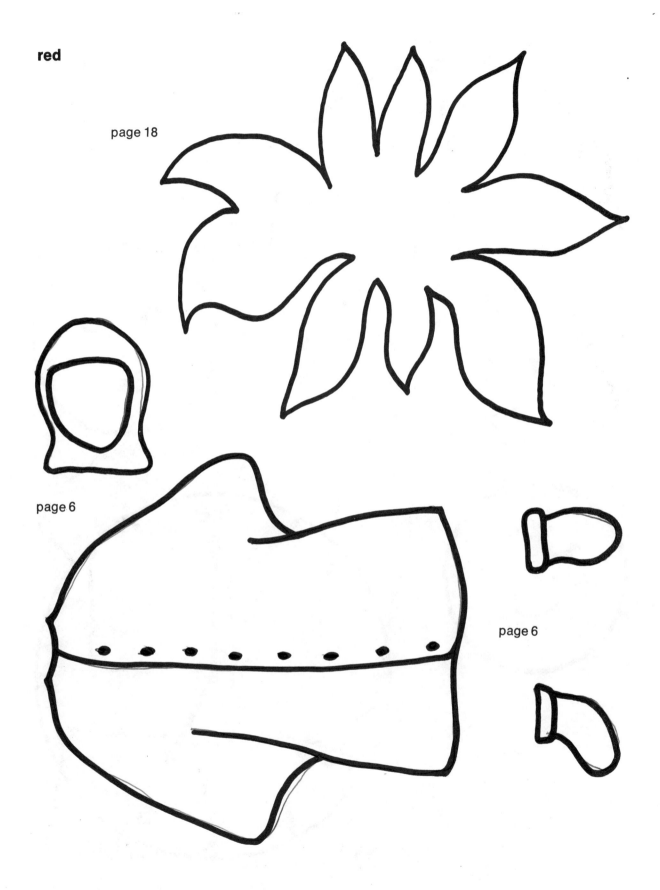

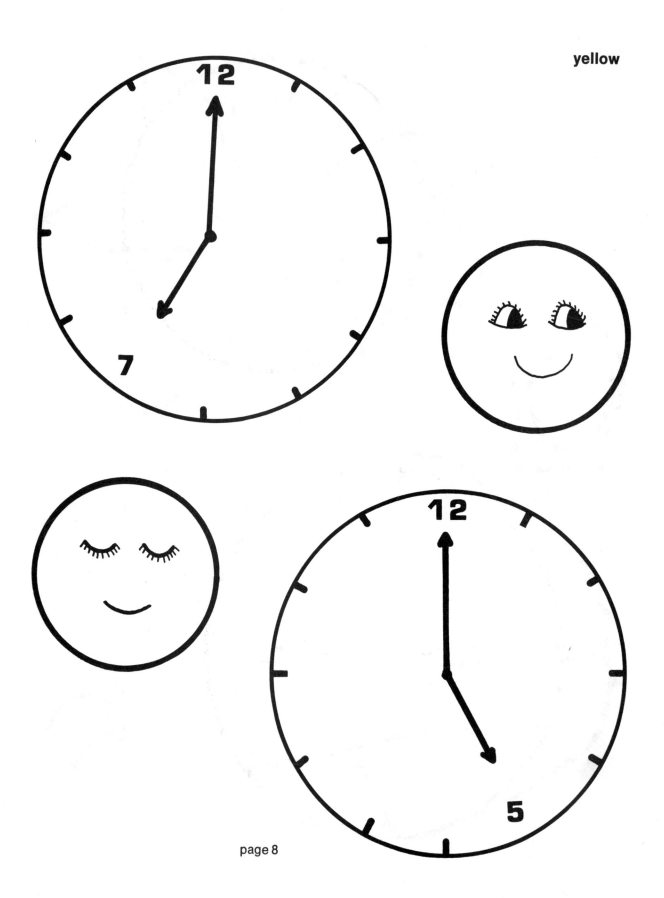

page 8

white

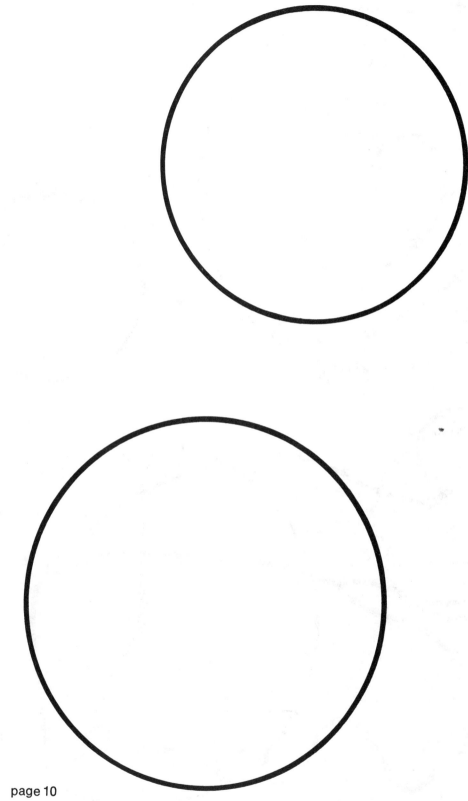

page 10

gray

page 16

page 12

48

green

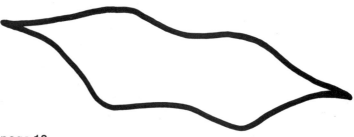

page 18

page 12

49

page 14

any color

page 16

page 20

UNIT III

Spring

Using the methods developed in earlier units, this unit will continue to make children aware of seasonal changes through lessons·about flowers, birds, animals, and weather changes in the spring. The emphasis is on the idea of the growth of new things in the spring.

The bulletin board should reflect the theme of the unit by showing a variety of pictures of blossoming trees and flowers, birds, spring weather conditions and so on. A weather chart that will be marked daily could also be posted.

The display table might include tree blossoms, cocoons and chrysalises, a thermometer, a rainfall gauge, an anemometer, and books and pictures having to do with spring. The gauges can be used outside after a demonstration on how they work.

The same materials that were used for the fall and winter booklets will be needed for making the spring booklet. *See* page 31 for a listing of these materials.

LESSON ONE

If you feel it is necessary, review the meaning of the word *season* before starting the day's discussion.

1. Ask what season has just gone by.
2. What season is just beginning?

3. What signs of spring do we see? (Blossoms and new leaves on trees. Grass is growing and getting greener. Flowers are beginning to grow from bulbs. It is time to plant seeds. Farmers are beginning to plow for spring planting. Birds are coming back and building nests to lay eggs in. Animals and some insects are coming out of hibernation. Insects are hatching from cocoons and chrysalises. The weather is changeable. It is getting warmer. The days are getting longer.)

4. Discuss how spring, especially March, is a good time for kite flying. Talk about Benjamin Franklin and his kite flying experiment. (Ben Franklin proved that lightning was electricity by flying a kite in a thunderstorm. He tied a metal key to the end of the string and the lightning traveled from the top of the kite down the wet string, causing a spark on the metal key.) Discuss how kites and airplanes stay up in the air. Tell about boy's kite day, May 5, when a carp-shaped kite is flown for each boy in the family.

By now, the children should understand about the title of a book, which is the front, and so on. But if they don't, repeat the review sequence outlined in Unit I.

Demonstrate how to compile the first two pages of the spring booklet. Cut out the boy and his jacket, hat, and pants. Paste the boy on page 2 and the clothes on the figure. Cut out the kite, paste it down, and draw a tail on it and a string from the boy's hand to the kite. Cut out the text for page 1 and paste it down. Read the text to the group and then supervise them as they cut and paste for their own booklets. Be sure to cut the art apart so that the children receive only the pieces they need for that day.

Art Project _____

Make a **fish kite** using one sheet of 18″ x 24″ newsprint and a fish pattern cut from tagboard. Fold the newsprint and place the fish pattern so that the bottom is on the fold as shown in the illustration. Trace around the pattern. Cut it out and staple the edges together. Paint scales on the fish with black poster paint and fill in the design using any two other colors.

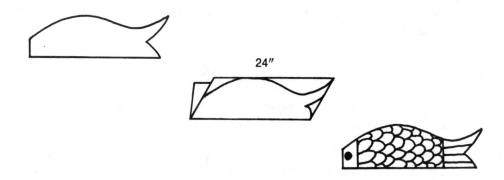

LESSON TWO

Review the previous lesson. Call on a volunteer to tell about the text in his booklet. Today discuss wind and air.

1. Ask what is air? Can we feel it? Taste it? Smell it? (Sometimes odors and smoke mix with air and we can smell it. Air takes up space. Blow up a balloon to show this. Have the children breathe deeply. Discuss how air fills their lungs.)
2. Who needs air? (All living things, including plants.)
3. Ask what is wind. (Moving air.) Does spring wind feel the same as winter wind? (No, it feels warmer.)
4. Can you think of other ways (in addition to flying kites) to have fun with the wind? (Sailing boats or using pinwheels, for example.)

Have the children cut out the text and paste it on page 3. Then they should cut out the sail and the boat and paste them down together on page 4 to make the sailboat.

Art Project _____

Have each child make his own **pinwheel.** Pass out duplicates of the pinwheel pattern and direct the children to cut along the lines. They should not cut all the way to the center. Show them how to fold each corner marked with an X to the center. Push a straight pin through the point of each corner as you fold it. Then push the pin through the center spot on the paper. Push the pin into an old crayon, a pencil stub, a short stick, or a sturdy straw. The children will need assistance from an older child or the teacher. When a child blows on his pinwheel or runs with it, it will turn.

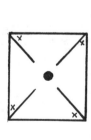 

LESSON THREE

Review the previous lessons and let the children take turns "reading" from their booklets. Then introduce today's lesson on the usefulness of the wind.

1. Ask if the children have ever heard of windmills. Discuss what windmills are and how they were used to pump water to irrigate fields, to grind corn, and to provide the power to run small mills. Show pictures of both steel and old-fashioned windmills, if possible.

2. Ask the children if they know of any particular country that is famous for its windmills. Talk about Holland, and perhaps tie the discussion to spring flowers, especially tulips.

3. Ask how people traveled over water before there were engines to make ships go. Talk about sailing ships, using pictures to make the discussion more meaningful. Show pictures of the *Mayflower* or Columbus' ships and discuss how long it took to cross the ocean on one of these ships versus how long it takes on a modern ocean liner.

Pass out the dittos of the windmill and arms and the text. Direct the boys and girls to cut out the windmill and blades. First, they should paste the windmill on page 6. Then, they should paste the arms at the top of the windmill. The text goes on the left-hand page.

LESSON FOUR

Review the previous lesson. Call on a volunteer to tell about the text in his booklet. Today discuss rainy weather.

1. Does it rain all the time where we live?

2. What seasons have the most rain?

3. Is it cold when it rains? (Sometimes—it is colder in the winter than in the spring. Spring rain is warmer than winter rain. It helps make the flowers and plants grow in the spring.)

4. Why do we need rain?

5. What is rain? (Water.)

6. Why is rain a good helper? (It washes things clean in the world. It waters everything—plants, trees. It keeps things from drying up. It fills lakes, rivers, oceans, etc. Rain gives us water for all our needs. All living things need rain in one form or another.)

7. Do we need special clothes for rain?

8. Where does rain come from? (Rain falls from the sky from clouds.) Sometimes we see rainbows when the sun shines through the water in the air after a rain. It is fun to listen to rain on the windows and the roof.

For the booklet, have the children cut out the cloud and paste it on the right-hand page. They can use a blue crayon to draw rain coming from the cloud. Each child can paste cotton on his cloud if desired. After they have cut apart the text and pasted it on page 7, read it to them.

Art Project _____

Make a **raindrop puppet** using the patterns for the body, arms, and legs found at the end of this unit. Cut out the patterns and assemble them with brads or a stapler. Punch a hole in the top of the puppet and put a string or a piece of yarn through the hole. Tie a knot in the string and use the puppet with a song about raindrops.

Raindrops

Rain- drops dance down to the ground, mak- ing pud- dles

as they dash. I put on my great big boots and

splash and splash and splash.

LESSON FIVE

After reviewing the previous lesson and having a child "read" from his booklet, introduce today's lesson on animals and insects.

1. Ask what is happening to the animals and insects that hibernated in the winter? (They are coming out of hibernation.)
2. Why do animals come out of hibernation in the spring? (Because the weather is getting warm and food supplies are more plentiful.)

3. When are baby animals born? When do insects hatch? (In the spring.) Show pictures of various animals and their young—bears, lions, deer, giraffes—or take a field trip to a local zoo.

Pass out duplicates of the text and the drawing of a mother bear and her cubs. Supervise the children as they cut out and paste the text on the left-hand page and the art on the right-hand page. Read the text to them.

LESSON SIX

Follow the usual procedure for review before starting the day's lesson on birds.

1. Ask the children if they remember what season the birds flew south.
2. **Review** why the birds flew south in the fall.
3. Point out that birds begin to return in the spring. Discuss why this is true. (Because the weather is warmer and food supplies are becoming plentiful.) One of the first birds to come back is the bluebird. Bluebirds are known for being peaceful and not fighting with other birds.
4. **Talk** about nesting. Ask the children where they think a good place for a nest would be. Explain that bluebirds like to build their nests in hollow trees or in birdhouses. The nest is made of grass.
5. Ask if the children have ever seen a red-winged blackbird. Explain that this bird has a red patch and a yellow patch on his wings. Show a picture if possible.
6. Where does this bird like to live? (Among cattails and bushes on the edges of streams or swampy places or in orchards under the trees. The female builds the nest, which may be in the reeds or cattails or on the ground. She lines the nest with soft grasses to hold the three to five eggs that she will lay.)

The children should cut out the text and paste it on the left-hand page. The blackbird should be ditted on white paper and colored or painted black. The patches on his wings should be colored red and yellow as indicated. The children can draw feet on their birds if they wish.

Art Projects _____

A **bluebird** can be constructed from a toilet tissue tube and blue construction paper. Use the blue paper to make a head, tail, and two wings, and to cover the tube. The base of the head and tail should be slightly wider than the tube. Make slits in the top and bottom of the tube at one end. Insert the head. Slit each side of the tube and insert the wings. Then slit each side of the end of the tube and slide in the tail.

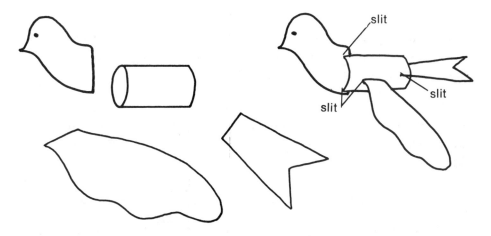

Make a **blackbird** in the same way, using black construction paper. Let the children color in the wing patch (or paste it on using red and yellow construction paper) if they want to have a red-winged blackbird. If they want their birds to be Brewer's blackbirds, they should color the eyes yellow.

LESSON SEVEN

Review the previous day's lesson and let the children take turns "reading" some of the booklet pages. Discuss again the fact that birds are returning. Today talk about the robin.

1. Ask the children why it is called "robin redbreast." Point out that the male bird has a redder chest than the female. You might wish to explain in more detail that most female birds are not as brightly colored as males. Show some pictures of robins, bluebirds, cardinals, goldfinches, and other birds common to your area to illustrate this.

2. What does a robin use to build her nest? (Twigs, string, mud, feathers, grass. Twigs and grass are used for a platform, and the walls are made of mud and more grass. She smooths the inside of the nest by turning around and around in the nest. She lines the nest with grass and feathers to make a soft bed for the eggs. They build their nests in tall bushes or trees so they will be safe from dogs and cats.)

3. Ask the group what color robin's-egg blue is. Talk about eggs and the incubation process. (The robin lays three or four eggs that hatch in eleven to fourteen days. The mother sits on the nest while the father bird stands guard.)

4. How do the baby birds get food? (When the babies hatch, both the mother and the father help to feed them. They find small insects, worms, and berries and feed them to their young until the baby birds are old enough to learn to fly and find their own food.)

5. Teach the class the robin song.

The Robin

Come, build in our tree, O
Rob- in red- breast. I'll give a mud- pie to
help build your nest, some string and some feath- ers
soft as can be. O Rob- in, dear Rob- in come
build in our tree.

Cut out and paste the robin on page 14 of the booklet and the text on page 13. The children may want to draw feet on their birds and a branch for the bird to sit on.

LESSON EIGHT

Review the previous lesson and the text in the booklet. Today discuss bulbs and flowers.

1. Ask the children if they remember what a bulb is and what it looks like. Review what kinds of flowers grow from bulbs.
2. When did we plant bulbs. (In the fall.)
3. Where have they been? (In the ground, "sleeping.")
4. What is happening to them now? (They are sprouting and growing.)
5. When do we plant seeds to grow other kinds of flowers? (In the spring or summer.)
6. What do seeds and bulbs need to make them germinate? (Explain that *germinate* means to sprout and grow. Seeds and bulbs need rain, sun, and warm weather.)

Have the children cut out and paste the tulip and the accompanying text in their booklets. Read the text to them.

Using the pattern found at the end of this unit, make a **three-dimensional tulip.** Duplicate the patterns for each child and give each a sheet of 9″ x 12″ blue or black construction paper. They should cut out the tulip, crease it on the lines, fold it around, and paste it together. Then direct them to cut out the stem and leaves, crease the leaves, and paste both leaves and stem on the blue or black construction paper. Paste the tulip at the top of the stem.

To make a **spring flower wall hanging,** arrange a thin strip of green paper in a curve on a 6″ x 18″ piece of white or black construction paper. Duplicate the flower patterns provided at the back of this unit on tagboard. Cut out the shapes and use them as patterns, tracing them on several colors of construction paper. Cut out the flowers and make a pleasing arrangement along the green strip. Paste the flowers in place. A three-dimensional effect can be achieved by bending the flower petals up and layering the flowers one on top of another. Use the leaf patterns provided at the end of the unit to make leaves that can be added to the wall hanging.

LESSON NINE

Review the previous lesson and text in the usual manner. Tell the children that today they will learn about farmers and spring planting.

1. Ask if anyone has ever lived on a farm.
2. What is _produce?_ (Fruits and vegetables.)
3. Where do stores get their produce? (From ranchers and farmers.)
4. What does a farmer do to the ground before he plants seeds? (He plows it.) Discuss the meaning of _plow._
5. Why are seeds planted in the spring? (It is too cold in winter; the ground is frozen in many places. Most vegetables and fruits must have all spring and all the warm summer to grow and ripen.)

Have the children cut out and assemble the geometric shapes (circles, rectangle, and square) to make the tractor. They should paste these on page 18 and draw the farmer sitting on the tractor. The text goes on page 17.

LESSON TEN

Review the previous lesson. Let the children take turns "reading" some of the booklet pages. Then discuss where fruit grows.

1. Ask the children if they can name some states where fruit grows. (Use a map to show where different fruits come from: Oranges are grown in Florida, Arizona, and California; peaches, in Georgia, California, South Carolina, Pennsylvania, and Michigan; pears, in California, Washington, Oregon, Michigan, and New York; apricots, in California, Washington, and Utah; apples, in Washington, New York, Virginia, California, Michigan, Pennsylvania, West Virginia, New Jersey, Ohio, and Massachusetts.)

2. Does fruit always grow on trees? (Berries, grapes, and tomatoes grow on vines.)

3. In the spring, fruit trees get blossoms first, then leaves. What are the blossoms for? (Blossoms become fruit.)

4. How do leaves help the fruit? (Leaves shade the fruit and keep it from getting too much sun.)

5. What does *ripe* mean? (Fruit starts out small and green. As it gets ripe, it grows and turns the proper color, showing that it is ready to be picked and eaten.)

Supervise the children as they cut out and paste the tree trunk in their booklets. To make the blossoms, they should dab pink or white paint on with swabs or straws. The accompanying text goes on page 19.

Art Projects ———————————————————————

Make another **blooming fruit tree** of brown yarn and crepe paper. Draw the outline of a tree trunk and branches on a piece of 9" x 12" blue or black construction paper. Cut brown rug yarn into different lengths and paste strands next to each other within the trunk outline. The yarn should fan out to become branches. Cut pink, white, and lavender crepe paper into small pieces approximately 1" x 1½". Twist the crepe paper to look like blossoms and paste the twists on the branches.

March 21 is the first day of spring.

In March, the weather changes a lot.

Some days are sunny and warm.

Some days are rainy and cold.

Sometimes the wind blows and blows.

It is fun to fly kites in March.

---------------------------- cut here—page 1 ----------------------------

THE WIND

The big wind pushed and pulled on me.

As he went whooshing by.

He blew my hat into the air.

And made my kite go high.

The wind helps you sail your sailboat, too.

It blows on the sail and makes the boat go.

When there is no wind, your sailboat will not move.

---------------------------- cut here—page 3 ----------------------------

Windmills are used to pump water from wells.
The wind makes the windmill's big flat arms turn.
When the arms go around, they make a pump go.
This pumps water up from the well.
The water is used for watering the fields.

------------------------------ cut here—page 5 ------------------------------

All living things need rain.
In the winter, rain is cold when you feel it.
In the spring, rain is warmer.
Rain helps flowers, vegetables, trees, and plants grow.
It fills the rivers, lakes, and oceans, too.

------------------------------ cut here—page 7 ------------------------------

In the spring, the animals that have been hibernating all
    winter are waking up.
They are coming out of hibernation.
Some of the mother animals have new babies with them.
This mother bear has two new cubs.

------------------------------ cut here—page 9 ------------------------------

This is a red-winged blackbird.
This pretty bird builds its nest near streams or swamps.
Sometimes it builds in orchards, too.
You will start to see this bird again in March.

------------------------------ cut here—page 11 ------------------------------

ROBIN REDBREAST

A robin redbreast
Built a nest
High up in my tree.
He used some strings
And sticks and things
And mudpies made by me!

------------------------------ cut here—page 13 ----------------------------------

Now it is spring.
The bulbs that we planted in the fall are beginning to grow.
Flower buds and green leaves are coming up through the
    ground.
This poem tells about two kinds of spring flowers.

SPRING FLOWERS

Daffodils march in a row.
And nod their yellow heads.
Tulips dance and bend down low.
In all my flower beds.

------------------------------ cut here—page 15 ----------------------------------

In the spring, farmers begin to plant seeds.

Vegetables, wheat, and other grains grow from the seeds.

First, the farmers must plow the ground.

Then, they can plant the seeds.

Farmers sell their produce to the store for your mothers
to buy.

-------------------------------cut here—page 17-------------------------------

Fruit trees blossom in the spring.

The pink and white blossoms are pretty to see.

One fruit grows from each blossom.

At first, the fruit is very tiny and green.

Then it begins to grow and get ripe.

-------------------------------cut here—page 19-------------------------------

any color

page 2

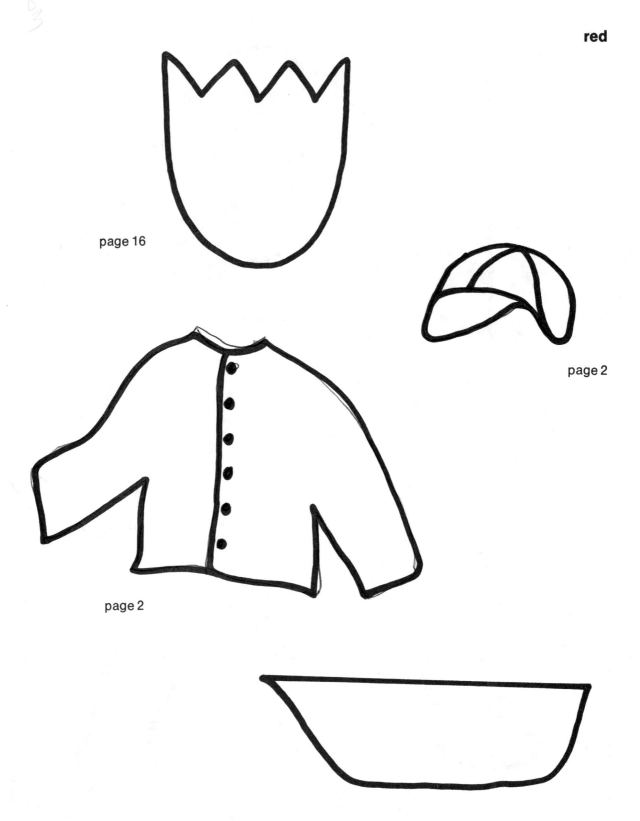

page 16

page 2

page 2

page 4

green

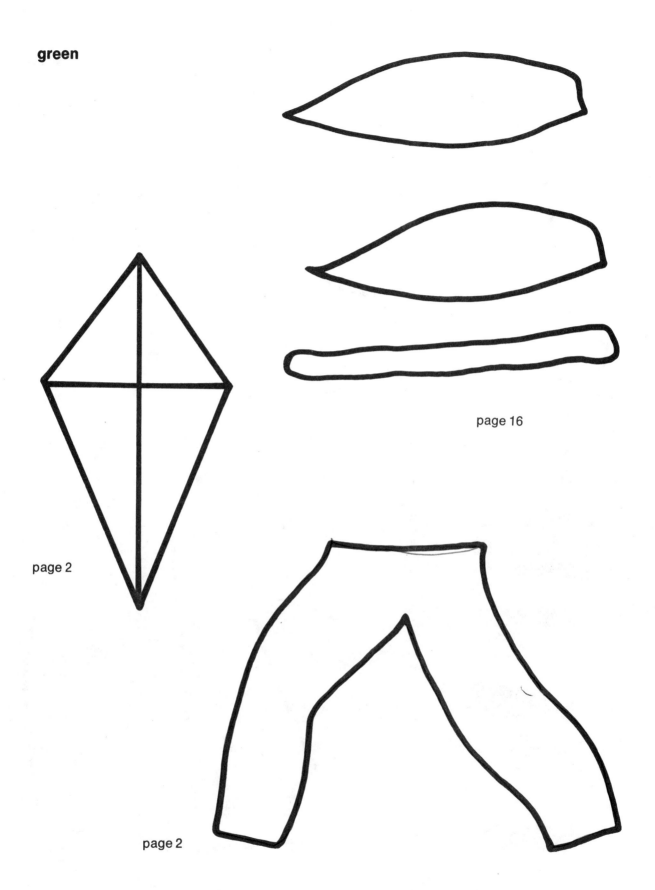

page 16

page 2

page 2

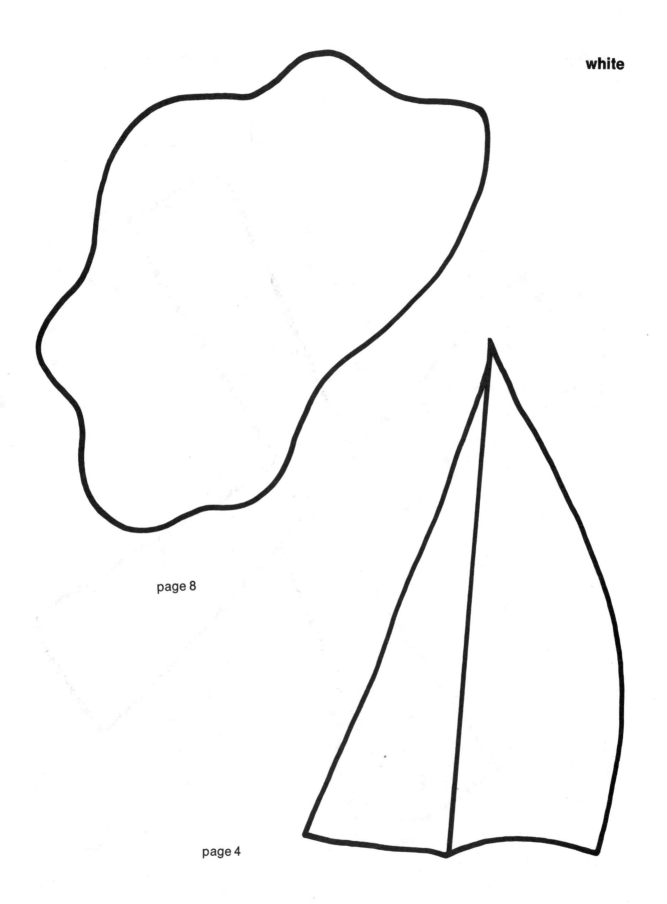

white

page 8

page 4

any color

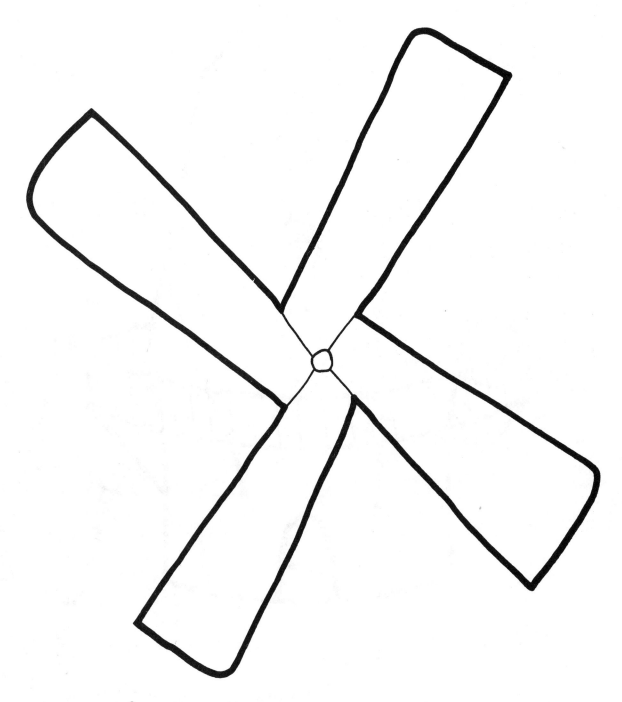

page 6

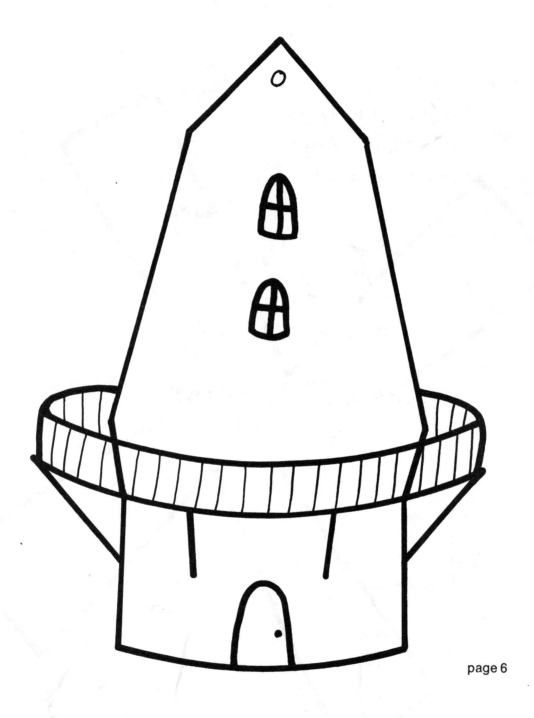

page 6

brown

page 10

73

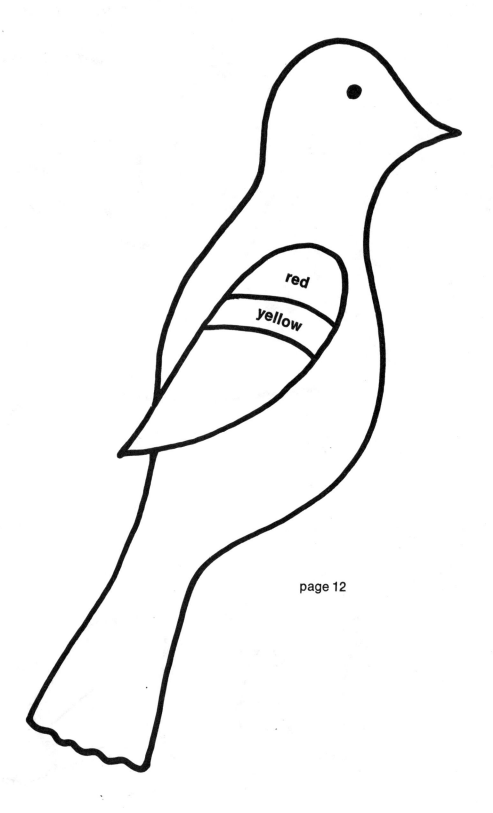

red

yellow

page 12

brown

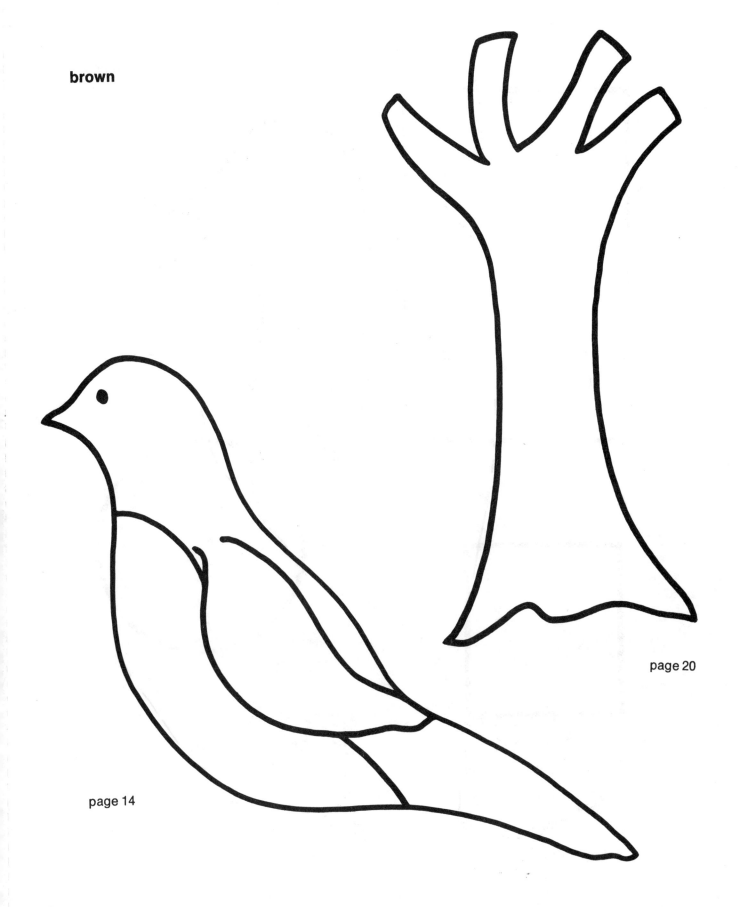

page 20

page 14

75

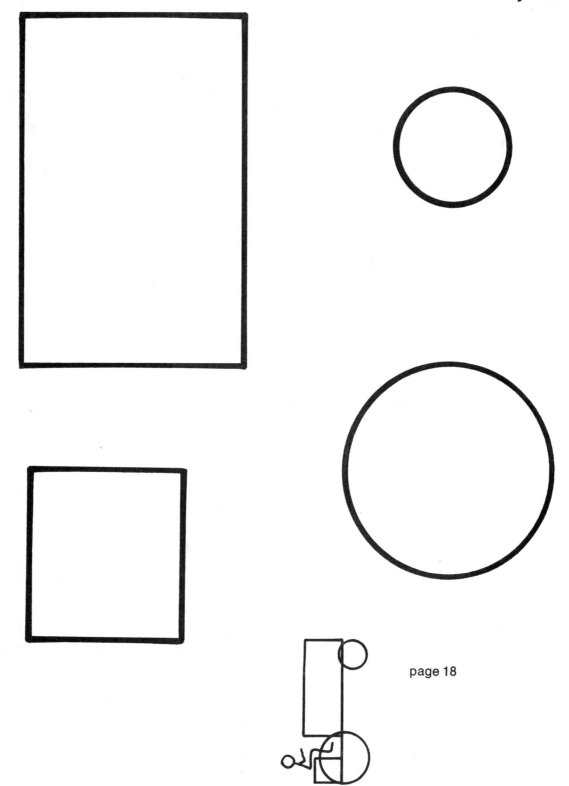

yellow

page 18

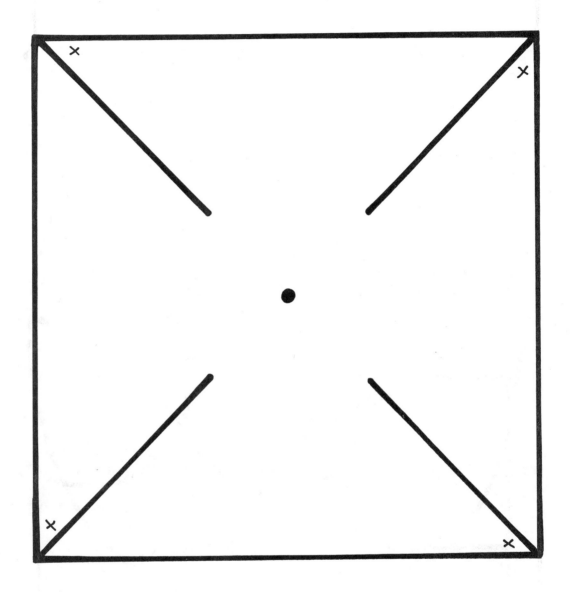

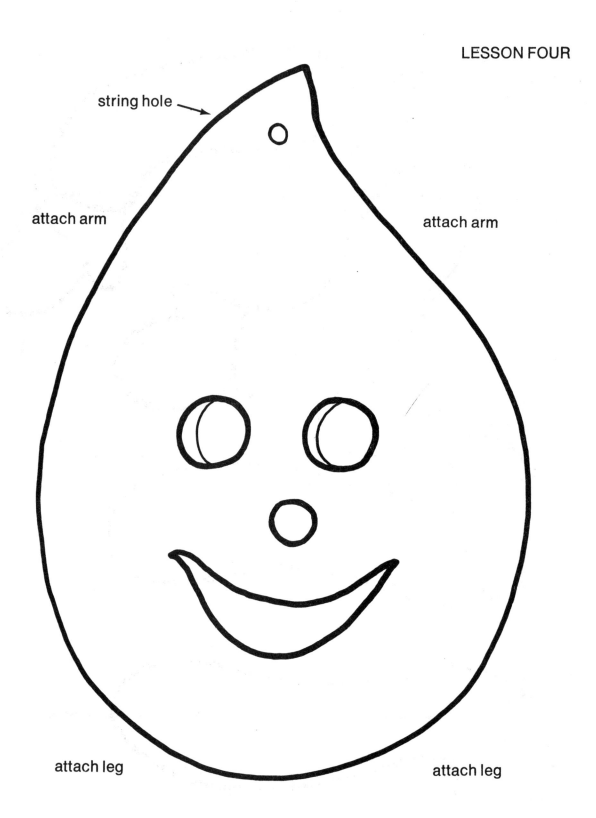

string hole

attach arm

attach arm

attach leg

attach leg

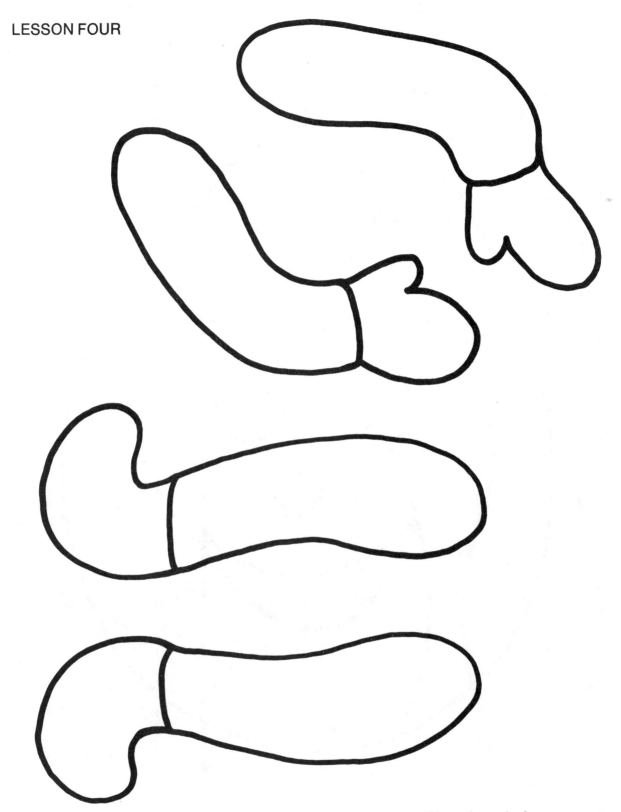

arms and legs for raindrop puppet

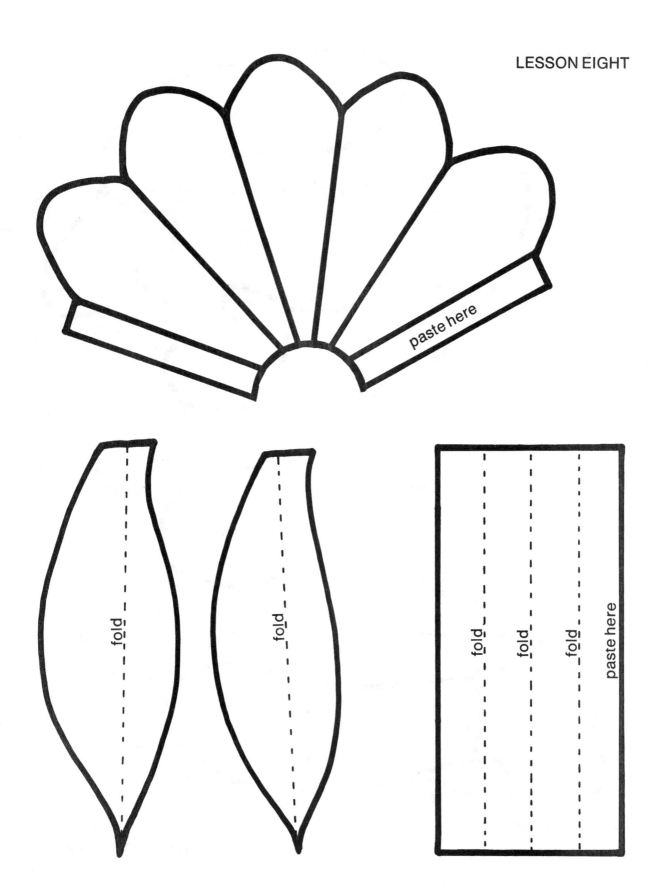

paste here

fold

fold

fold

fold

fold

paste here

UNIT IV

Summer Vacation

The purpose of this unit is to make children aware of the world around them and to help them know what to look for when on trips to the park, the mountains, or the beach.

The bulletin board for this unit should feature pictures that show typical scenes of summer recreation available in your area.

The display table should hold many objects that the children can handle. For example, shells, starfish, beach equipment such as a pail and shovel, pinecones, and even small camping equipment could be displayed.

Prepare blank booklets for the number of children in your class. See page 31 for a listing of the materials needed. The illustrations found at the end of this unit should be duplicated on construction paper and the text on ditto paper. Both should be passed out daily.

LESSON ONE

Introduce the idea of summertime as vacationtime by asking a few questions.

1. What is a vacation? (Time off from work or school when we can relax and have fun.)

2. What can we do on a vacation? Where can we go? (Take trips, swim, play, go to the park, to the mountains, the beach, grandmother's house, and so on.)
3. Do we need to leave home to have fun? What can we do if we stay home? (Go to the zoo, go to the park, go on picnics, play baseball, go wading or swimming, ride bicycles.)
4. What is the weather like in summer?

Pass out the booklets to each child. Have the children write the title of the booklet—"Summer Vacation"—on the cover. Follow the established procedure for introducing the booklet. Then pass out duplicates of the text and illustration. Demonstrate and then have the children cut out and paste the text on page 1 and the wading pool on page 2. Each child should draw a picture of himself in the pool and color the pool any color he chooses. Read the text to the children.

LESSON TWO

Review the previous lesson. Let a child open his booklet and "read" the first page. Today talk about camping as a way to spend a vacation.

1. Have you ever been camping?
2. What do we mean by camping? (Sleeping outdoors in a tent or camper. Cooking food outdoors.)
3. What must we take on a camping trip? (Sleeping bags, air mattresses, old clothes, food, firewood, cook stove, pans, dishes, silverware, cooler, lantern.)
4. Where would it be fun to go?
5. Why is it nice to be able to sleep in a tent, trailer, or camper? (We would be protected from rain, wind, and insects.)

Each day, demonstrate the lesson assembly in your own booklet before handing out the materials. Then pass out duplicates of the illustration and text and let the children cut out the tent, trailer, and camper. They should paste them on the right-hand page and put the correct text on the left.

LESSON THREE

Review the previous lesson and let the children take turns "reading" from their booklets. Then talk about how camping in the mountains is fun. Review what equipment is necessary and add a heater to the list.

1. When we go camping, what do we sleep in? (Sleeping bags or folded blankets.)

2. Talk about campfires. Explain that a campfire should be built in the place provided at the campsite, the barbecue pit for example. Some camping areas allow fires on the ground if you dig a fire pit and put a ring of rocks around the fire. What is a campfire used for? (Cooking, toasting marshmallows, warmth. It is fun to sit around a campfire after dinner and talk or tell stories.)

3. What should you do to a campfire when you go to bed and when you leave the campground? (Put it out thoroughly by putting water and dirt on it.)

4. What happens when campers are careless with campfires? (They may start a forest fire which would burn many trees, driving many animals from their homes and killing some of them.) Should boys and girls play with fire?

Stress using the next page in the booklet, demonstrating with your own booklet. Have the children cut out the sleeping bag, paste it on the right-hand page, and then cut out the paper doll and insert it into the sleeping bag. The text should be pasted on page 5.

LESSON FOUR

Review the previous lesson. Let the children take turns "reading" the text from their booklets.

1. What kinds of small creatures might we see in the mountains? (Chipmunks, squirrels, lizards, snakes.)

2. What do chipmunks look like? (They are smaller than a squirrel, reddish brown with black and white stripes down their backs, and have skinny tails.)

3. Where do they live? (In a burrow under the ground.) Discuss the word *burrow*.

4. What kinds of large animals might we see in the mountains? (Bears, deer.)

5. Should we try to pet or feed a bear? (No.) Why? (It is dangerous to get near bears. Bears are big and strong and can claw people. If you do not bother bears, they will not bother you.)

6. Do bears sometimes come around campgrounds at night? (Yes, because they are hungry. They come after food that people have left out, or they get into garbage cans.)

Have the group cut out and paste the chipmunk onto page 8 and the text on page 7. If desired, have them draw the stripes down the chipmunk. Read the text to them.

LESSON FIVE

Review the previous lesson. Let the children take turns "reading" from their booklets. Today discuss deer.

1. Ask where deer live. (In the woods.)
2. Has anyone ever seen a deer?
3. When do they come out? (Mostly at night. Deer are very shy animals.)
4. Mother, father, and young deer all have different names. Does anyone know what they are called? (Doe, buck, fawn.)

Supervise the children as they cut out and paste the deer on page 10 of their booklets and the text on page 9.

LESSON SIX

Follow the usual procedure for reviewing the previous lesson. Tell the children that today you are going to talk about a trip to the beach.

1. What should we take? (Bathing suit, beach towel, beach ball, sand pail, shovel, suntan lotion.)
2. What can we do at the beach? (Swim, play in the sand, play ball.)
3. What is a beach made of? (Fine or coarse sand, pebbles, rocks.)
4. What kinds of things can we look for at the beach? (Different kinds of shells and rocks, for example. In the shallow pools we can find many kinds of sea creatures, including starfish.)
5. Has anyone ever seen a starfish? How many legs do starfish have? (Five.)
6. How do they stick to the rocks? (They have hundreds of small feet on each leg. On each foot is a suction cup.) Bring in a suction cup and show the children how it works so they will understand the principle.

Let the children cut out the starfish and paste it on the right-hand page. The text goes on page 11.

Shells, starfish, and other sea creatures are available from several sources. Two such sources are listed here. The teacher should inquire about rates and the availability of materials.

The Gulf Specimen Company	Shell Shop
Jack J. Rudloe, Director	Edna Nelson
P.O. Box 237	P.O. Box 43
Panacea, FL 32346	Port Aransas, TX 78373

LESSON SEVEN

After reviewing the previous lesson, continue the discussion about the seashore.

1. What other unusual creatures do we see in the shallow water or on the beach? (Crabs, crayfish, jellyfish, for example.)
2. Have you ever seen a crab? Crabs are queer-looking creatures. They walk sideways. Their eyes are on ends of stems on the front of their bodies. They have a hard shell. They have five pairs of legs. The first pair has claws or pincers on the ends.
3. Are crabs good to eat? Have you ever eaten crab?
4. Ask if anyone has ever found a clam at the beach. Discuss clamming and how pearls are developed. Show the children a pearl and an open clam shell, if possible.

The children should cut out the crab and paste it on page 14 of their booklets. The text goes on page 13.

LESSON EIGHT

Today discuss beach birds, after first reviewing yesterday's lesson.

1. What kinds of birds might you see when you go to the beach? (Sea gulls, pelicans, terns, sanderlings, sandpipers, curlews, for example.)
2. What color is a sea gull? (White with black or gray markings. Their bills are usually yellow, and some gulls have a red spot on the lower bill.)
3. What is a *scavenger?* Discuss the meaning of this word. (Sea gulls are scavengers. They are the garbage men of the sea. They follow boats and eat the waste thrown overboard. They also help keep the beaches clean by eating garbage and dead fish.)
4. Where do they build their nests? (Gulls nest in colonies or large groups. Most build on cliffs above the ocean, but some build nests closer to the ground and water. They usually lay about four or five eggs.)

Supervise as the children cut out the gull and paste it on page 16. The text goes on page 15.

LESSON NINE

Review the previous lesson and let the children take turns "reading" from their booklets.

1. Ask if anyone knows what a pelican looks like. (Very large birds with heavy bodies, long necks, large yellow or grayish bills, white or brown

feathers. The white pelican is about five feet long and has a wing span of eight to ten feet.)

2. Where would you see pelicans? (Near water.)
3. What do pelicans eat? (Fish.)
4. How do pelicans catch fish? (Brown pelicans dive into the water and scoop fish into the expandable pouch on their bills. White pelicans scare fish by beating the water with their wings. Both scoop fish up with the bills, and the large pouch under the lower bill expands to hold the fish. The pelicans stop fishing to drain off the water from their pouches. Then they tip their heads back and the fish slide down their throats. Pelicans always eat the fish immediately; they never store them in their pouches for a long period of time.)

The children should paste the text on page 17 and cut out and paste the pelican on page 18. Read the text to them before going on to the next lesson. The child may color the pelican's feet and bill if they want.

LESSON TEN

Follow the customary review procedure and then begin the discussion about turtles.

1. Ask if anyone has a turtle for a pet. Explain that some turtles live on land and that some live in the water. Tell the children that turtles come in all different sizes and that there are many different kinds. Small turtles that live in water have webbed feet and larger turtles have flippers.
2. Discuss turtles that live in the sea. Use a map to point out where the turtles live. (They live where the ocean is warm, off the coast of Florida and the West Indies, for example.) Some turtles are large enough to ride on. They have strong jaws and can be dangerous, though.
3. Do you think turtles build nests? Where do you think the mother turtle lays her eggs? (She comes out of the water and lays hundreds of eggs in the sand.)
4. Does she sit on them until they hatch? (No. She buries them in the hot sand and the sun warms them until they hatch. It takes about two months for the eggs to hatch.)
5. Where do baby turtles go after hatching? (They crawl down to the sea and swim away. They must take care of themselves as soon as they hatch. The female left after burying eggs two months earlier.)

Pass out the duplicates of the turtle and the text. The children should cut out and paste the turtle on page 20 and paste the text on page 19.

Everybody likes a vacation.

It is a time to have fun.

People do anything they want on a vacation.

They may stay home and do things around the house.

They may take a trip to the mountains, the beach, the city, or the country.

They may take a trip to visit someone, too.

-----------------------------cut here—page 1----------------------------------

It is fun to go camping.

What do you take with you?

Some people use a tent.

Others drive a camper truck or pull a trailer.

-----------------------------cut here—page 3----------------------------------

What do you sleep in when you go camping?

A sleeping bag is a good thing to have.

If you do not have a sleeping bag, you can fold warm blankets to make one.

-----------------------------cut here—page 5----------------------------------

Chipmunks look a little like squirrels.

But they are smaller and their tails are not bushy.

They are reddish brown and have black and white stripes
down their backs.

They like to eat berries and nuts.

Sometimes they are so tame that they will eat from your hand.

-------------------------------- cut here—page 7 --------------------------------

Have you ever seen some deer while you were camping?

They are very shy.

Deer hide during the day and come out at night for food and
water.

-------------------------------- cut here—page 9 --------------------------------

You may see a starfish at the beach.

A starfish has five legs and is shaped like a star.

He has little suction cups underneath his legs to help him
stick to the rocks.

His mouth is in the center of his body.

Starfish live in shallow pools at the seashore.

-------------------------------- cut here—page 11 --------------------------------

There are many things to see at the beach.

Many sea creatures live in the shallow water near the shore.

You may see crabs in the water and on the shore.

Crabs are many different sizes.

It is fun to watch a crab move because he walks sideways.

-------------------------------- cut here—page 13 ---------------------------------

Sea gulls are large white and gray birds.

They eat almost anything.

Gulls like to follow boats and eat the food and fish scraps
   that are thrown overboard.

Sometimes they rob the nests of other birds.

They also eat small fish that they catch in their bills.

By eating dead fish and trash left on the beach, gulls help
   keep beaches clean.

-------------------------------- cut here—page 15 ---------------------------------

This is a brown pelican.

He dives into the water and scoops fish into his pouch.

He drains the water out through his bill.

Then he tips his head back and the fish slide down his throat.

-------------------------------- cut here—page 17 ---------------------------------

The sea turtle lays her eggs in the sand.

She covers the eggs up with sand and leaves them there.

The sun warms the sand so that the baby turtles hatch.

After the baby turtles hatch, they go down to the sea and swim away.

Some sea turtles grow so large that they could hold a child on their backs.

------------------------------ cut here—page 19 ------------------------------

white

page 6

page 2

page 4

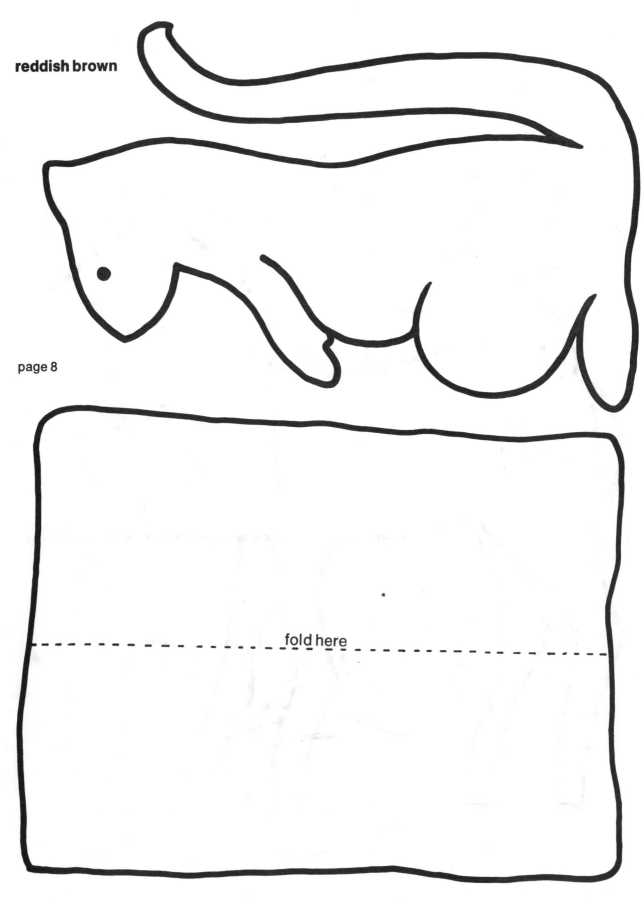

reddish brown

page 8

fold here

page 6

95

page 10

brown

page 12

page 14

white or gray

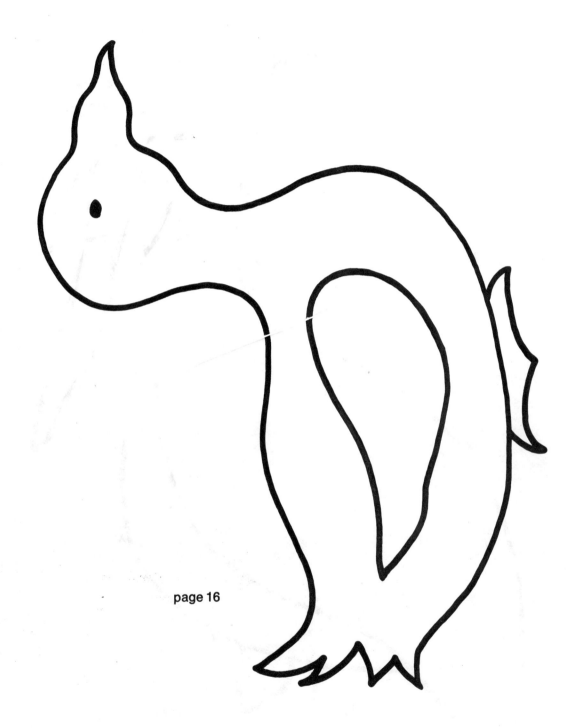

page 16

brown

page 18

green

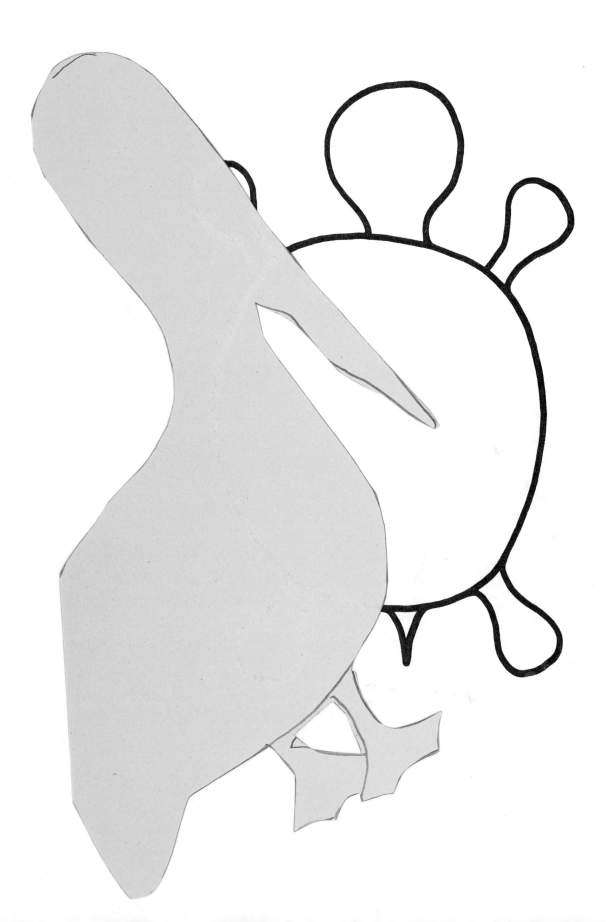

Bibliography

BOOKS

Fall

Aliki, Brandonburg. *Story of Johnny Appleseed*. Englewood Cliffs, N. J.: Prentice-Hall, Inc., 1963.

Lenski, Lois. *Now It's Fall*. New York: Henry Z. Walck, Inc., 1948.

Miller, Edna. *Mousekin's Golden House*. Englewood Cliffs, N. J.: Prentice-Hall, Inc., 1964.

Norman, Gertrude. *Johnny Appleseed*. New York: G.P. Putnam's Sons, 1960.

Peterson, John. *Tulips*. New York: Holt, Rinehart & Winston, Inc., 1963.

Salten, Felix. *Perri*. Racine, Wisc.: Western Publishing Company, Inc., 1957.

Tresselt, Alvin. *Autumn Harvest*. New York: Lothrop, Lee & Shepard Co., Inc., 1951.

Winter

Burton, Virginia. *Katy and the Big Snow*. Boston: Houghton Mifflin Company, 1943.

Eitzen, Allen. *Birds in Winter*. New York: Holt, Rinehart & Winston, Inc., 1963.

Frosty the Snowman. Retold by Annie North Bedford. Racine, Wisc.: Western Publishing Company, Inc., 1950.

Hoban, Lillian. *Some Snow Said Hello*. New York: Harper & Row, Publishers, 1963.

Kay, Helen. *One Mitten Louis*. New York: Lothrop, Lee & Shepard Co., 1960.

———. *Snow Birthday*. New York: Farrar, Straus & Giroux, 1955.

Keats, Ezra Jack. *Snowy Day*. New York: The Viking Press, Inc., 1962.

Krauss, Ruth. *The Happy Day*. New York: Harper & Row, Publishers, 1949.

Lenski, Lois. *Now It's Winter*. New York: Henry Z. Walck, Inc., 1950.

McKié, Roy, and Eastman, P.D. New York: Random House, Inc., 1962.

Munn, Ian. *Johnny and the Birds*. Chicago: Rand McNally & Co., 1950.

Schlein, Miriam. *The Sun, the Wind, the Sea, and the Rain*. New York: Abelard-Schuman Limited, 1960.

Shulevitz, Uri. *Rain Rain Rivers*. New York: Farrar, Straus & Giroux, 1969.

Slobodkin, Florence and Louis. *Too Many Mittens*. New York: Vanguard Press, Inc., 1958.

Tresselt, Alvin. *The Mitten*. New York: Lothrop, Lee & Shepard Co., Inc., 1964.

———. *White Snow, Bright Snow*. New York: Lothrop, Lee & Shepard Co., Inc., 1947.

Yashima, Taro. *Umbrella*. New York: The Viking Press, Inc., 1958.

Spring

Fritz, Jean. *Late Spring*. New York: Coward, McCann & Geoghegan, Inc., 1957.

Carrick, Carol. *Swamp Spring*. New York: The Macmillan Company, 1969.

Gottlieb, William. *The Four Seasons*. New York: Simon & Schuster, Inc., 1957.

Henderson, L. M. *A Child's Book of Birds*. New York: Maxton Books, 1946.

Kohler, Cynthia Iliff and Alvin. *The Wonder Book of Birds*. New York: Wonder-Treasure Books, 1961.

Lenski, Lois. *Spring Is Here*. New York: Henry Z. Walck, Inc., 1945.

Shapp, Martha and Charles. *Let's Find Out About Spring*. New York: Franklin Watts, Inc., 1963.

Tresselt, Alvin. *Hi, Mister Robin!* New York: Lothrop, Lee & Shepard Co., Inc., 1950.

Wiese, Kurt. *Fish in the Air*. New York: The Viking Press, Inc., 1948.

Summer

Berenstain, Stan and Jan. *The Bear's Picnic*. New York: Random House, Inc., 1968.

Gottlieb, William. *The Four Seasons*. New York: Simon & Schuster, Inc., 1957.

Lenski, Lois. *On a Summer Day*. New York: Henry Z. Walck, Inc., 1953.

Schick, Eleanor. *City in the Summer*. New York: The Macmillan Company, 1969.

MUSIC

Fall

Burnham, Maude, and Wood, Lucille F. "The Owl and the Brownies," *Singing Fun*. Manchester, Mo.: Webster Division, McGraw-Hill, 1954.

Kapp, Paul. "One Fine October Morning," *A Cat Came Fiddling*. New York: Harcourt Brace Jovanovich, Inc., 1956.

Milne, A.A., and Fraser-Simson, H. "Christopher Robin Is Going." *The Pooh Song Book*. New York: E.P. Dutton and Company, Inc., 1961.

Scott, Louise B. "Falling Leaves," *Singing Fun*.

Winter

Milne, A.A., and Fraser-Simson, H. "The More It Snows," *The Pooh Song Book*. New York: E.P. Dutton and Company, Inc., 1961.

Reynolds, Malvina. "Little Birds," *Cheerful Tunes for Lutes and Spoons*. Berkeley, Calif.: Shroder Music Co., 1970.

Wood, Lucille F., and Franke, Kathryn. "Walking Weather," *Singing Fun*. Manchester, Mo.: Webster Division, McGraw-Hill, 1954.

———, and Scott, Louise B. "Funny Snowman," *Singing Fun*.

Spring

Burnham, Maude, and Scott, Lousie B. "Green Frog," *Singing Fun*. Manchester, Mo.: Webster Division, McGraw-Hill, 1954.

Favelka, Virginia. "Springtime," *Singing Fun*.

Guthry, Woody. "Little Seed," *Songs To Grow On*. New York: William Sloane Associates, Inc., Publishers, 1950.

Kapp, Paul. "For It Is a Pleasant Day," *A Cat Came Fiddling*. New York: Harcourt Brace Jovanovich, Inc., 1956.

———. "Spring Is Coming," *A Cat Came Fiddling*.

Milne, A.A., and Fraser-Simson, H. "Oh, the Butterflies Are Flying," *The Pooh Song Book*. New York: E.P. Dutton and Company, Inc., 1961.

Ritchie, Jean. "May Carol," *Jean Ritchie's Swapping Song Book*. New York: Henry Z. Walck, Inc., 1964.

Traditional. "Birds' Courting Song," *Songs To Grow On*.

Traditional. "Pussy Willow," *Singing Fun*.

Wood, Lucille F., and Scott, Louise B. "Springtime." *Singing Fun*.

Summer

Burnham, Maude, and Scott, Louise B. "A Green Frog," *Singing Fun*. Manchester, Mo., Webster Division, McGraw-Hill, 1954.

Kapp, Paul. "Did You Ever Go Fishing?" *A Cat Came Fiddling*. New York: Harcourt Brace Jovanovich, Inc., 1956.

Rainey, Marguerita. "Seashore," *More Singing Fun*. Manchester, Mo., Webster Division, McGraw-Hill, Inc., 1961.

Reynolds, Malvina. "All Over Everything," *Cheerful Tunes for Lutes and Spoons*. Berkeley, Calif.: Shroder Music Co., 1970.

Traditional. "Over in the Meadow," *Children's Songs*. New York: Simon & Schuster, Inc., 1966.

Wood, Lucille F. "Ice Cream Man," *More Singing Fun*.

————. "Lonely Little Sailboat," *More Singing Fun*.

FILMS

Fall

Animal Homes (Churchill Films; 11 minutes; color; 1954).

Animals in Autumn (Encyclopedia Britannica Educational Corp.; 11 minutes; color; 1957.)

Autumn Is an Adventure (Coronet Films; 11 minutes; color; 1952.)

Blow Wind, Blow (Coronet Films, 11 minutes; color; 1952).

Children in Autumn (Encyclopedia Britannica Educational Corp.; 10 minutes; color; 1958).

How Seeds Are Scattered (Encyclopedia Britannica Educational Corp.; 10 minutes; color; 1958).

Winter

Animals in Winter (Encyclopedia Britannica Educational Corp.; 11 minutes; black and white; 1950).

Children in Winter (Encyclopedia Britannica Educational Corp.; 11 minutes; color; 1958).

Play in the Snow (Encyclopedia Britannica Educational Corp.; 11 minutes; black and white; 1945).

Winter Is an Adventure (Coronet Films; 11 minutes; black and white; 1954).

Spring

Animals in Spring (Encyclopedia Britannica Educational Corp.; 11 minutes; color; 1955).

Children in Spring (Encyclopedia Britannica Educational Corp.; 11 minutes; color; 1958).

The Robin (Dan Gibson Productions; 6 minutes; color; 1966).

Robin Redbreast (Encyclopedia Britannica Educational Corp.; 11 minutes; black and white; 1957).

Spring Is an Adventure (Coronet Films; 11 minutes; black and white; 1955).

Summer

Animals in Summer (Encyclopedia Britannica Educational Corp.; 11 minutes; color; 1954).

Black Bear Twins (Encyclopedia Britannica Educational Corp.; 10 minutes; black and white; 1953).

Children in Summer (Encyclopedia Britannica Educational Corp.; 11 minutes; color; 1957).

Common Animals of the Woods (Encyclopedia Britannica Educational Corp.; 11 minutes; black and white; 1943).

How Trees Help Us (Coronet Films; 11 minutes; color; 1957).

Life on a Dead Tree (Film Association of California; 11 minutes; color; 1957).

Seashore Life (Encyclopedia Britannica Educational Corp.; 10 minutes; color; 1950).

We Explore the Field and Meadow (Coronet Films; 11 minutes; black and white; 1961).

We Explore the Stream (Coronet Films; 11 minutes; color; 1960).

Wonders in Your Own Backyard (Churchill Films; 11 minutes; color; 1948).

FILM INDEX

Churchill Films, 662 N. Robertson Blvd., Los Angeles, Calif. 90069.

Coronet Films, 65 E. South Water Street, Coronet Bldg., Chicago, Ill. 60601.

Encyclopedia Britannica Educational Corp., 425 North Michigan Ave., Chicago, Ill. 60611.

Film Association of California, 11559 Santa Monica Blvd., Los Angeles, Calif. 90025.

Dan Gibson Productions, 291 Delaware Ave., Buffalo, N.Y. 14202.